THE MORE THINGS CHANGE ...

HUMAN RIGHTS IN HAITI

February 1989

Americas Watch
The National Coalition for Haitian Refugees
Caribbean Rights

Photos by Carol Halebian/Gamma-Liason

Front cover: Residents of Port-au-Prince examine campaign posters at headquarters of Haitian Christian Democratic Party (November 1987).

Back cover: Headquarters of National Agricultural and Industrial Party in Port-au-Prince (November 1987). The banner reads: "A people without a memory is a people without a future."

Cover design by Charlotte Staub

This report is available for $10.00 from:

Americas Watch   National Coalition or Haitian Refugees
36 West 44th Street   or   275 7th Avenue
New York, NY 10036   New York, NY 10001

We dedicate this report to Michael S. Hooper, our cherished friend, whose unparalleled devotion to human rights in Haiti and commitment to Haitians fleeing abuses in their country will always serve as an inspiration to those of us who seek to continue his work.

Table of Contents

ACKNOWLEDGMENTS

This is the eighth report on human rights in Haiti issued by Americas Watch and the National Coalition for Haitian Refugees (NCHR) since 1983. This report covers events since the issuance of the last report by these two organizations in mid-November 1987, *Haiti: Terror and the 1987 Elections.* Joining them in issuing this report is Caribbean Rights, a coalition of seven nongovernmental human rights organizations from the Caribbean.

The report is based in substantial part on seven fact-finding missions to Haiti. In November-December 1987, Americas Watch and NCHR established an "Election Watch" office in Haiti for the purpose of monitoring human rights conditions surrounding the scheduled national elections of November 29. The office was manned by Michael S. Hooper, then Executive Director of NCHR, and Jocelyn McCalla, then Associate Director and now Executive Director of NCHR. During the days immediately surrounding the elections, they were joined by two representatives of Americas Watch, Kenneth Roth, Deputy Director of Human Rights Watch, and Stanley Engelstein, a member of the board of directors of Americas Watch; and two representatives of Caribbean Rights, Frank Solomon, an attorney from Trinidad and Tobago, and Msgr. Jan Caulewaert, a Roman Catholic Bishop from Belgium who is associated with Pax Christi International.

Hooper returned to Haiti in January 1988 to monitor the human rights conditions surrounding the substitute national elections called for January 17. The mission was Hooper's last for our organizations; after many years of dedicated and invaluable service, he died of cancer in September at the age of 41.

In May 1988, McCalla traveled to Haiti to look into random killings and other abuses committed during the presidency of Leslie Manigat.

In August 1988, a six-member delegation traveled to Haiti to investigate the deteriorating human rights situation under then President Lt. Gen. Henri Namphy. The delegation was composed of Roth; McCalla; Marina Kaufman, a member of the board of directors of Americas Watch; Josh DeWind, a member of the board of directors of NCHR; Michael McCormack, Executive Secretary of Caribbean Rights; and Paulo Sergio Pinheiro, coordinator of the Sao Paulo Human Rights Commission of the Federal Bar Association of Brazil. The delegation was assisted during portions of its investigation by Maryse Fontus, who joined Human Rights Watch in September as its Orville Schell Fellow.

Since Lt. Gen. Prosper Avril assumed the presidency, McCalla and Anne Fuller, Assistant Director of NCHR, traveled to Haiti in November 1988; McCalla returned in December 1988; and Fuller visited again in January 1989.

Fuller, McCalla, Fontus, Kaufman and Roth contributed to the writing of this report. '

* * * * *

The National Coalition for Haitian Refugees is comprised of 47 legal, human rights, civil rights, church, labor and Haitian community organizations working together to seek justice for Haitian refugees in the United States and to monitor and promote human rights in Haiti. Its Executive Director is Jocelyn McCalla and its Assistant Director is Anne Fuller.

Americas Watch was established in 1981 to monitor and promote observance of free expression and other internationally recognized human rights in Central America, South America and the Caribbean. The Chairman is Adrian W. DeWind and the Vice Chairmen are Aryeh Neier and Stephen Kass. The staff consists of Juan E. Mendez, Executive Director; Cynthia Brown, Associate Director; Jemera Rone, Counsel; Anne Manuel, Reports Editor; and Mary Jane Camejo, Research Associate.

Americas Watch is part of Human Rights Watch, which also includes Africa Watch, Asia Watch and Helsinki Watch. The Executive Committee of Human Rights Watch consists of: Robert L. Bernstein, Chairman; Adrian W. DeWind, Vice Chairman; Roland Algrant, Dorothy Cullman, Jack Greenberg, Alice H. Henkin, Stephen Kass, Jeri Laber,* Aryeh Neier,* Matthew Nimetz, Bruce Rabb and Kenneth Roth.* Its staff consists of: Aryeh Neier, Executive

---

*   ex-officio.

Director; Kenneth Roth, Deputy Director; Holly Burkhalter, Associate Director; Wendy Luers, Special Projects Director; Susan Osnos, Press Director; and Joanna Weschler, Prisoner Watch Coordinator.

Caribbean Rights is composed of human rights organizations from the Bahamas, Belize, Guyana, Haiti, Jamaica, Puerto Rico, and St. Vincent and the Grenadines, with headquarters in Barbados. Its Executive Secretary is Michael McCormack and its Coordinator is Wendy Singh.

The authors wish to thank the following Haitian human rights organizations for their assistance: the Ecumenical Center for Human Rights, the Haitian Center for Human Rights, the Haitian League for Human Rights, the Institute for Democratic Education, the Karl Leveque Center, and the League of Former Political Prisoners.

Copies of this report are available for $10.00 from:

Human Rights Watch
36 West 44th Street
New York, New York 10036
(212) 840-9460

or

The National Coalition for Haitian Refugees
275 Seventh Avenue
New York, New York 10001
(212) 741-6152

I. INTRODUCTION

Since the downfall of the Duvalier dictatorship three years ago, Haiti has been ruled by a series of military-dominated governments. Each, including the current government of Lt. Gen. Prosper Avril, has vowed to usher in democracy and respect human rights. Each, including the current one, has mocked these vows by its actions. Today, Haiti is little closer to an elected, lawful government than it was on February 7, 1986, when "President-for-Life" Jean-Claude Duvalier boarded a military transport plane for exile in France. Violence directed or tolerated by the army continues to be the government's principal medium for addressing the proliferation of popular organizations pressing for democratic change.

The governments, to be sure, have had different faces. And at various moments different factions of the army have been ascendant, frequently in conjunction with allied paramilitary forces. But behind the rotating governments, the changing facades and the competing military factions lies an unwavering refusal by the army to relinquish its grip on power, together with the opportunities for corruption which power has implied. The toll for maintaining this privileged position has been ongoing political violence and serious human rights abuses.

Gen. Avril, the current president, has been no exception to this disturbing consistency. Among Haitian democrats and the human rights community, the cautious optimism that greeted Gen. Avril's rise to power in a September 1988 coup has given way to deepening disappointment, as the Avril government increasingly adopts the repressive practices of its predecessors. Although Gen. Avril remains verbally committed to democratic changes, he has proved unwilling to break with the reactionary forces that stand opposed to popular rule.

This unwillingness cannot be explained by lack of opportunity. Gen. Avril was brought to power by a group of noncommissioned officers who took umbrage at the ascendancy and increasingly brazen violence of paramilitary forces operating under the protection of Lt. Gen. Henri Namphy and his allies. These soldiers continue to press for reforms and would be natural allies of a government that acted to promote democracy and human rights.

Instead, Gen. Avril imprisoned fifteen of their leaders, holding them for over two months without charge or trial, on unsubstantiated allegations of plotting a coup. He has reinstated corrupt and violent commanders who had been ousted by their troops. And he has halted significant efforts to disband the paramilitary forces that have played a major role in the most violent episodes in Haiti's recent past.

Large segments of the democratic opposition also greeted Gen. Avril's rise to power with offers of dialogue and cooperation in moving toward elections and building respect for human rights. Gen. Avril has pursued a dialogue with these groups and has vowed to permit an independent electoral commission to run elections. But he has not yet endorsed the full set of electoral terms contained in the popularly enacted Constitution of March 1987, and he has refused even to recognize the Constitution as a legally binding instrument. Meanwhile, he has countenanced violence against critics and popular organizations, increasingly suggesting an intention to maintain military control of any future elected government. These actions have added to the polarization of Haitian society, leading growing numbers to doubt that an Avril government can be trusted to hold free and fair elections.

This report covers the period since shortly before the crushed elections of November 29, 1987. In the fifteen months since then, despite periodic fluctuations, there has been a disturbing persistence in the nature and intensity of serious abuses. The report reaches the following conclusions:

- Violence is regularly used by the army and its paramilitary allies to discourage and at times prevent collective political activity. The most common targets have been the popular organizations of the sort that precipitated the ouster of the Duvalier dictatorship and have since led the opposition to the various military-dominated governments: peasant organizations, trade unions and the progressive church. Anti-government demonstrations are also routinely dispersed, particularly outside Port-au-Prince. Among the more deadly examples of this practice have

2

been the September 1988 attack on St. Jean Bosco church in Port-au-Prince, which left a dozen dead and over 70 wounded, and the August 1988 attack on a peasant youth group in Labadie, which left four dead.

- Violence has also been used against outspoken opponents of the government. Lafontant Joseph, a leading human rights attorney, was killed in July 1988 in circumstances suggesting military involvement. Luc B. Innocent, a vocal critic, was killed by an army patrol in October 1988. Michelet Dubreus and Jean Félix, who issued a public letter identifying participants in the St. Jean Bosco massacre, were promptly murdered by armed men led by a uniformed soldier in November 1988.

- Torture and killing in police custody continues, particularly in the Criminal Investigations Unit of the Port-au-Prince Police Department *(Service des Recherches Criminelles)*, renamed the Anti-Gang Investigations Bureau *(Service d'Investigations Anti-Gangs)* by the Avril government. At least through September 1988, inmates in *Recherches Criminelles* regularly died from torture or starvation, and severe beatings were routinely practiced. Although the Avril government claims to have stopped detaining prisoners in the facility, approximately 40 were being held there as recently as January 1989, and reports of beatings and at least one killing have emerged.

- Troops continue to use deadly force against the population-at-large with seeming impunity. The problem is most pronounced among rural section chiefs *(chefs de sections)*, particularly in the Artibonite region in central Haiti. Even within Port-au-Prince, killings and robberies increasingly are committed by uniformed soldiers.

- This disregard for the rule of law has encouraged a resurgence of what Haitians call "insecurity," the killing of seemingly random citizens by unidentified gunmen. Reflecting an apparent attempt to terrorize the population, bodies continue to appear periodically on the streets of Port-au-Prince.

- Neither the Avril government nor its predecessors have made any headway in bringing to justice the perpetrators of the many political killings and other abuses that have continued to plague Haiti since the fall of Duvalier. No prosecutions have been brought and no convictions have been obtained for a single act of political violence. To the contrary, at the end of December 1988, the Avril government issued a safe conduct out of the country to former Col. Franck Romain, a close as-

3

sociate of ousted Gen. Namphy, who is widely believed to have engineered the St. Jean Bosco massacre.

- The few announced investigations into political murders have ended in whitewash. In November 1988, the Avril government issued a report on the August 1987 murder of presidential candidate Louis Eugene Athis and his two aides which said that the victims should have known better than to campaign in the area where they were killed; the widely acknowledged mastermind of the killings, section chief David Philogene, was released from protective custody and allowed to flee to the Dominican Republic. Also in November 1988, the Avril government issued a report on the November 1987 election day massacre which failed to identify a single participant in the killings. Popular outrage at the report led the government to propose a new investigative commission, but procedural constraints imposed by the government on the proposed commission, such as a requirement that it complete its work in one month, led Haitian human rights groups to reject the proposal, and no further action has been taken. No new investigation was even proposed into the Athis murder.

- At the request of the democratic groups which participated in a forum organized by the government, Gen. Avril has agreed to establish an independent electoral council to run elections at a still-unspecified date. Although the proposed council is modeled after the electoral council called for by the Haitian Constitution, Gen. Avril has not reinstated the widely popular constitutional provision barring from public office for ten years those who were architects of the Duvalier dictatorship, embezzled public funds or engaged in torture or murder of political opponents. It remains to be seen whether a new electoral law will incorporate this constitutional provision and whether it will ensure the genuine independence of the electoral council.

- Quite apart from the laws and institutions established to organize elections, future elections in Haiti are threatened by ongoing political violence. The lesson of the failed November 1987 elections is that voting cannot be expected to proceed while the army sponsors and tolerates political violence and intimidation. Until politcal attacks are stopped, paramilitary forces are disarmed and security is assured, there is little likelihood that free and fair elections can proceed.

- The Haitian press, particularly the all-important radio stations, continue to be the targets of violence. Although certain radio stations, such as the Catholic Church's Radio Soleil and the private Radio Haïti-

Inter, are particularly courageous in their willingness to report on politically sensitive topics, self-censorship is prevalent in light of periodic military and paramilitary assaults.

- By cutting off most direct aid to the Haitian government following the collapsed elections of November 1987, the United States provided a powerful incentive for the Haitian military to embark on a democratic and lawful path. Leading democrats and human rights monitors in Haiti believe that they would now have little leverage to persuade the army to reform if military leaders did not perceive that the renewal of aid depended on respect for human rights and the holding of free and fair elections. Unfortunately, on two occasions in 1988, the Reagan administration undercut this stance by approving loan guarantees totaling $19 million to U.S. exporters. The guarantees allowed commercial sales to the Haitian government to go forward, permitting the government to resell the commodities at a profit and thus generate desperately needed revenues at a time when the effects of the aid suspension were being acutely felt.

- The U.S. embassy in Port-au-Prince under Ambassador Brunson McKinley has wasted its considerable moral influence by remaining largely silent in the face of ongoing abuses. Rather than speaking out consistently against human rights violations, Ambassador McKinley has adopted a hurt silence since his plans for trusting the military to permit elections exploded in the election day massacre of November 1987. In an August 1988 interview with our investigative mission to Haiti, Ambassador McKinley excused his failure to protest abuses with the quip that "repetition becomes boring," called human rights violations "endemic to the Haitian tradition," and referred to the Haitian countryside as governed by "the law of the jungle."

It is not too late for the Haitian military to change its direction. The initial popular reaction to the September 1988 coup showed a Haitian population eager to embrace the army if it acts to promote democracy and defend human rights. Although polarization has grown in the five months since that coup, there remains an important and respected role for the army to play -- subordinate to elected civilian authorities and respectful of human rights, but contributing actively and significantly to the pressing task of raising Haiti from its deepening poverty.

It is unfortunate that those who have headed the Haitian army in the last three years have not had the vision to assume this role. They have not seen the collapse of the Duvalier dictatorship as an opportunity for reform, but remain entrenched in the corrupt and violent ways of the past, ready to sacrifice the political and economic future of the nation for the rewards of profit and plunder.

We call on the Haitian military government to commit itself to uphold democracy and respect human rights. Unlike the empty promises of the past, however, we call on the military government to back up these vows with concrete actions, including by:

- ordering a halt to all political violence by the military and those working in concert with it;
- commencing aggressive and impartial investigations into all instances of political violence, including those of the past, and prosecuting all perpetrators before fair and public tribunals;
- disarming paramilitary forces, both those attached to the army and those operating independently, including by aggressively seeking out and seizing weapons caches;
- reinstating the March 1987 Constitution and publicly reaffirming the rights that are contained in it, including freedom of association and assembly; and
- establishing an independent electoral council according to the procedures outlined in the Constitution, agreeing to hold elections as soon as the independent council deems appropriate, providing protection for all electoral participants, permitting the elections to proceed freely and fairly without interference, and abiding by the results of the elections.

We also call on the US government to maintain the suspension of aid to the Haitian government until it takes the steps outlined above, and to ensure that the purpose of this aid suspension is not undercut by funding provided through indirect channels. And we urge the US, especially its embassy in Port-au-Prince, to abandon its policy of silence by becoming a forceful and outspoken voice protesting all serious abuses and actively pressing for democracy and respect for human rights.

Finally, we call on the international community to direct its attention to the persistent abuses in Haiti and to exert its influence on the military government to cease the violent obstruction of democratic aspirations. The United Nations Commission on Human Rights should begin public scrutiny of human rights practices in Haiti by appointing a special rapporteur, with the aim of curtailing abuses by exposing them and their perpetrators to world condemnation. In addition, international donors to Haiti should ensure that no money is delivered to or passed through the Haitian military government until that military has relinquished power to an elected, civilian successor and has ceased violating fundamental human rights.

II. ATTEMPTS TO CONTROL THE ELECTORAL PROCESS

On November 29, 1987, as the world watched, Haiti's presidential elections -- the long-hailed centerpiece of its transition to democracy -- drowned in a sea of blood, leaving Haiti more firmly than ever under the control of the military and its Duvalierist allies. The tragedy for Haiti, where at least 34 people died and 75 were wounded, was also a humiliating defeat for United States policy. The Reagan administration had pushed the National Governing Council *(Conseil National de Gouvernement)* (CNG) to pledge support for democratic elections in which it had no interest, paid the government's bills with doubled foreign aid, and overlooked the military's increasing violence, so long as the CNG remained officially committed to holding elections.

The popular movement that had sprung up since Duvalier's departure saw the elections as a way to make a break with the Duvalierist past, an opportunity for change. To these forces, the holding of elections was more important than the politics of particular candidates. The most popular candidates (according to a pre-election poll and returns from the first few hours of voting on November 29) were those who had stood up to the Duvalier dictatorship: Sylvio Claude, a Protestant Minister who had been jailed numerous times for his opposition activities; Gerard Gourgue, the long-time human rights activist; Louis Déjoie II, the son of a former opponent of the late Francois Duvalier; and Marc Bazin, who had tried to clean up corruption in the Duvalier government.

Under the Duvaliers, the army had been kept at arms length from real power by its rival, the Tontons Macoutes. Now, with Duvalier gone, the army was in charge. Democratic groups in Haiti believed that pressure from allies overseas who demonstrated support for the elections, particularly when backed by the threat of a loss of aid, would be sufficient to push the CNG to live up to its stated commitment to hold elections. These hopes were not without historical precedent. Haiti had been expected to follow the Latin American trend of military dictatorships giving way to civilian administrations. In the case of

9

Haiti, however, international pressure was not forthcoming. When the Reagan administration reacted to the campaign of anti-election terror and obstruction with no more than a shake of its finger, the CNG believed it could do as it pleased. And it did.

A. Accelerating Violence

As outlined at greater length in the last report by the National Coalition for Haitian Refugees and Americas Watch, *Haiti: Terror and the 1987 Elections* (November 1987), there were many early signs that the Namphy government was fundamentally opposed to free and fair elections. The CNG first tried to control the electoral process by stacking with its own supporters the constituent assembly that was to draw up a new constitution. Surprisingly, however, that body produced a draft constitution which called for elections to be run by an electoral commission that was independent of the military. The draft constitution also barred from public office for ten years "architects" of the Duvalier dictatorship as well as those who had embezzled public funds or tortured or murdered political opponents. These provisions led to the adoption of the Constitution by an overwhelming majority: 98.99% of the approximately 1.2 million voters in a referendum on March 29, 1987.

Faced with the prospect of a genuinely independent body to run the elections, the Provisional Electoral Council *(Conseil Electoral Provisoire)* (CEP), the CNG attempted, through legal maneuvers, to dominate the group and limit its powers. On June 22, 1987, the CNG issued a decree that superseded the CEP's proposed electoral law with one giving responsibility for running the elections to the CNG. At a press conference, Information and Coordination Minister Jacques Lorthé announced: "Whether the CNG decree is constitutional or not does not matter to us."

But when this move was met by international outrage and a widely supported general strike, the Namphy government backed down, only to unleash its new strategy: a return to the naked terror of the Duvalier days. The army took to shooting peaceful demonstrators, and death squads began leaving mutilated bodies on the streets of Port-au-Prince.

During the week of June 22, 1987, at least 35 persons were shot dead in random attacks.* Deadly attacks on peaceful demonstrators continued in July and August. And on August 2, one presidential candidate, Louis Eugene Athis, was stoned and hacked to death by a mob led by the local section chief, David Philogène, in the town of Léogàne.

Upon occasional U.S. demand, the CNG still intoned its commitment to elections, but it was an empty pledge designed to cover up a campaign of terror aimed at discouraging participation in the elections. The emptiness was only reinforced by the willingness of the Reagan administration to focus on words instead of deeds. In the midst of the terror campaign, on July 23, 1987, U.S. Deputy Assistant Secretary of State for Inter-American Affairs Richard Holwill testified before the Senate Foreign Relations Committee that the CNG had "consistently stressed its commitment to the democratic transition" and had "on balance" fulfilled its "contract with the Haitian people to deliver elections." By contrast, in testimony at the same hearing the National Coalition for Haitian Refugees and Americas Watch predicted more army repression unless the U.S. halted military aid to the CNG and insisted on demonstrated respect for human rights before approving aid of any sort. Nonetheless, on August 26, 1987, the State Department certified to Congress that Haiti's human rights situation was improving, placing its seal of approval on the army's violence of the previous two months as it made the requisite finding to continue military aid.

In mid-October 1987, another presidential candidate, Yves Volel, was shot in the head at close range by police detectives. The murder took place directly in front of the headquarters of the Criminal Investigations Unit *(Service des Recherches Criminelles)* of the Port-au-Prince Police Department, in full view of a group of Haitian and foreign journalists. The State Department deplored the killing but failed to note the police involvement.

When the CEP on November 2 applied the anti-Duvalierist provision of the Constitution, Article 291, and ruled 12 Duvalierist presidential candidates ineligible, renewed terror was unleashed. Twelve armed men blocked off the

---

*   This figure was derived from visits by our representative to the public morgue, as well as from official records of the University of Haiti Hospital.

street in front of the headquarters of the CEP, located just a few hundred yards from police headquarters and the Casernes Dessalines, Haiti's largest military barracks. They fired rounds of ammunition into the air to scare off passersby, chiseled through heavy metal shutters to enter the premises, and set fire to the building, destroying most of the CEP's records. Not a single police officer or soldier responded to the attack.

That same night the offices of Continental Trading, a business owned by CEP member Emmanuel Ambroise, were also destroyed by fire. The Departmental Election Bureau, responsible for the voting in the Department of the West which includes Port-au-Prince, was attacked by machine guns. Throughout the night gangs of men in civilian clothes drove around the city, spraying gunfire in all directions. Two days later, one of the three printing presses that were being used to print election materials -- ballots, voter registration cards and voter education leaflets -- was destroyed in an arson attack.

No arrests were made in connection with any of this violence. The CEP had made numerous requests to the government for protection, but none was heeded. Only after CEP headquarters were burned down was an armed guard supplied.

On November 6, 1987, when Gen. Namphy appointed himself to a three-year term as commander-in-chief of the army (an appointment that under the Constitution should have been made by the elected president), he made no mention of the violence but praised the army for "having always been consistent." The only apparent "consistency" was the army's antipathy to the elections.

Attacks on candidates, election volunteers and local CEP offices continued on a regular basis throughout November. On November 25 in Gonaïves, for instance, 200 armed men paraded through the streets and shot up the local electoral office. On November 27, in the rural town of Borel in the central Artibonite region, soldiers in a jeep opened fire on the home of senatorial candidate Victor Benoit, killing three peasant bystanders, including a secondary school student; at least 12 people were also detained. Haitian human rights monitors estimate that during this period an average of two or three bodies were found each day on the streets of Port-au-Prince, with most of the killing performed under cover of night.

The terror motivated residents of Port-au-Prince's poorest neighborhoods to form self-defense committees *(brigades de vigilance),* which blocked access to communities at night. On November 23, one such committee killed a man caught with gasoline which it believed he was planning to use to set fire to a market. The previous day, November 22, arsonists had destroyed the capital's third largest open-air market, the Marché Solomon. Two other men said to have taken part in election-related violence were also beaten to death by self-defense committees.

Whereas the military government and the police had ignored the dozens of earlier deaths at the hands of military and paramilitary forces, these actions by neighborhood-based groups drew a prompt reaction from then Defense and Interior Minister Gen. Williams Régala. On November 25, he issued a communiqué warning the self-defense committees that keeping order was the "direct and exclusive" responsibility of the armed forces. "We will absolutely not tolerate any group that tries to substitute for the armed forces, who intend to carry out their duties by all possible means." The following morning, eight bodies were found on the streets of Port-au-Prince, one identified by Radio Métropole as a member of a neighborhood patrol group.

B. Logistical Obstructions

In addition to its role in this terror campaign, the CNG worked to obstruct the elections at a logistical level. It withheld all practical support from the CEP, kept back millions of dollars in US-donated funds for the elections until the very last minute, and denied the CEP television and radio time to explain election procedures. The CNG also refused the CEP use of army helicopters, which were needed to transport election material to Haiti's many remote villages. When the CEP leased two helicopters from a private Miami firm, the Interior Ministry denied them flight permission.

Given the climate of fear and terror that surrounded the attempt to carry out the elections, and the attendant logistical difficulties, it is not surprising that preparations for the planned elections were flawed. In the countryside, where the military and paramilitary forces operated most freely, few candidates dared to run for local posts. Local elections planned for July 1987 had to be postponed until mid-December 1987, and when by November 16 only 9 candidates had registered for 137 mayoral posts and 17 candidates for 565 positions on rural councils, the elections were simply cancelled.*

In contrast, even following the CEP's disqualification of 12 presidential candidates under the constitutional provision barring former Duvalierists from office, there remained 23 candidates for president, although a number of them had ludicrous platforms and no constituency. Under the procedures established for Haiti's largely illiterate population, each voter was supposed to receive and choose from a package of ballots, with a separate ballot for each candidate showing his name, picture and party emblem. That procedure required more than 60 million ballots for the presidential election alone. These problems, which would have been a challenge to the most experienced and well-funded electoral authority, were all the more difficult to surmount after the CEP's headquarters were burned down on November 2.

The CEP's achievements under these conditions were remarkable. Making use of a nationwide network of volunteers, the CEP in less than two months managed to register 2.2 million people, or 73 percent of Haiti's voting-age population.

Without helicopters and jeeps, election officials were forced to use the most primitive methods to reach the electorate. The director of the elections bureau for Port-au-Prince and its province told reporters two weeks before the vote that he had only one jeep and one motorcycle to cover the entire Western Department of Haiti. The ballots for the 56,000 residents of Cornillon, for example, located 30 miles from any road, had to travel three days by mule.

As election day approached, hundreds of journalists and international observers gathered in Haiti. Usually a substantial force for ensuring free and fair elections, these foreigners had little effect in weakening the determination of the Haitian military authorities to stop the process. Throughout the two days preceding November 29, some 15 armed men blocked cars carrying CEP offi-

---

*   On January 31, 1988, elections were held for these rural councils, known as Conseils d'-Administration des Sections Communales, or CASECS. The turnout was reportedly under five percent of registered voters.

14

cials, international observers and journalists along the main road connecting Port-au-Prince to the northern part of the country. They burned a truck carrying 200 boxes of ballots and brandished pistols at foreign travelers.

Alain Hertoghe, a reporter for the French Catholic daily *La Croix,* was part of a group that attempted to reach St. Marc. He recounted his experience on the road a few miles south of his destination:

"Suddenly, at a turn, a road block stopped us. Two men came toward the car brandishing machetes. At the same moment, a civilian pick-up truck full of soldiers was let through the barrier.

"My worried look meets nothing but indifference in the eyes of two soldiers seated in the back of the vehicle. Already the men with machetes are upon us, while the military abandons us to our fate....

"A group of some 20 men arrive, led by a big peasant man in a yellow t-shirt and armed with a pistol. One of the men brandishes a can of gasoline....

"'Let's burn the jeep!' says the one carrying the can, in the midst of the general commotion. The man with the revolver indicates that we should take off our shirts, which we do with the greatest calm, fear in our stomachs. 'Get back in the car!' he then shouts.

"All of a sudden, another man, taking out a revolver, forbids us from entering the vehicle. He forces my colleague to take out his [Nagra sound] recorder and give it to him. Twice he throws it on the ground, before striking it with the butt of his weapon. Finally, he decides to shoot it but his gun doesn't function.

"The representative from the Haitian Collective [*Collectif Haïti*] attempts to calm the situation by showing his Observer card. With a sharp gesture, the individual in the yellow t-shirt sticks his revolver under his chin. A third man also takes out a firearm. The machetes threaten. For an indeterminate moment I feel that our lives are in suspense.

"'Get in! Get in!' the man in the yellow t-shirt then shouts. Rapidly we get into the car. He makes a sign that we should leave. The car starts to move, while he runs, the revolver

15

pointed at Jean-Claude Patassini. Finally he stops, while the others shout 'Shoot! Shoot!' Very rapidly, we are out of range."

Because of this roadblock, the CEP was forced to postpone elections in five towns in the central Artibonite region, and few foreign journalists were able to witness the electoral process in the northern half of Haiti. Local election councils were also forced to postpone the polling in the Department of the North, which includes Haiti's second largest city, Cap Haïtien.

C. Election Day

During the early-morning hours of election day, November 29, 1987, Port-au-Prince crackled with steady gunfire and occasional explosions as bands of gunmen drove through the streets shooting randomly and setting fire to three local electoral offices and a gas station. According to witnesses, about 30 army soldiers launched a pre-dawn assault with automatic rifles and hand grenades on the home of CEP treasurer Alain Rocourt. "We saw whole handfuls of shells and seven used hand grenade clips," said an election observer, the Rev. Allan Kirton of the Caribbean Conference of Churches, who was inside Rocourt's house at mid-morning when troops returned to shower it again with gunfire.

At dawn at least seven bodies were found on the streets of Port-au-Prince. But in defiance of the terror, Haitians lined up outside polling places, which opened at 6 a.m.

In Petion-Ville, Delmas and Carrefours Feuilles, army troops fired into the air to intimidate would-be voters. Outside the capital the violence was widespread, but more difficult to monitor. In Gonaïves, troops invaded polling places, destroyed ballots and fired in the air to frighten away voters. In Les Cayes, Haiti's third largest city, soldiers also fired into the air to scare off voters.

The most bloody incident occurred at a downtown Port-au-Prince polling place in an elementary school called the Ecole Argentine de Bellegarde. Approximately 100 voters were in line at about 7:30 a.m. when at least 50 men carrying automatic rifles and machetes burst into the courtyard and fired at them. Witnesses said some of the attackers used their machetes to finish off the wounded who lay screaming in pain from their bullet wounds. At least 14 people were killed.

When minutes later a group of journalists arrived on the scene, they, too, were attacked. According to Jean-Bernard Diederich, a freelance photographer working for *Time* magazine, a grey jeep carrying helmeted army soldiers drove up to the door and the troops opened fire into the school's courtyard. The journalists fled under fire, leaping over walls and into people's homes to save themselves. Dominican cameraman Carlos Grullon was shot at close range and died at midday. Two members of an ABC News camera crew and their Haitian driver were shot by a uniformed gunman who followed them behind a wall where they had tried to hide, "took careful and deliberate aim," and fired at close range, according to ABC correspondent Peter Collins.

Election observers said paramilitary forces attacked at least three Catholic churches in Port-au-Prince, killing at least two worshippers. At one church, Sacre Coeur, which was doubling as a polling station, Father Nicholas Christian, the parish priest, reported that paramilitary troops interrupted the morning mass, beat two women with the butts of their machetes, climbed on the altar and destroyed several altar pieces.

Former U.S. Ambassador to El Salvador Robert White, an independent election observer, said he saw army troops remove a rock barricade put up by neighborhood residents and allow a band of paramilitary troops to pass. "The army totally abandoned its responsibility," he said. "It turned the streets over to the Macoutes."

In a written report on election-day violence in Haiti's central Artibonite region issued on December 1, 1987, the Justice and Peace Commission of the Roman Catholic Diocese of Gonaïves concluded that an operation "to stop the democratic elections" was, in the Artibonite, planned by the army and carried out with support from death squads and certain local Duvalierists. The army, the report noted, enlisted a full array of sophisticated weapons in this effort:

> "The arms used in the Artibonite directly against civilian objectives were semi-automatic weapons with very great firepower. Everywhere machine guns on stands, which are fired by pressing a pedal because of the force of the recoil, were deployed. The impact of these bullets on the presbytery of Petite Riviere measured more than 20 cm. in diameter. Wit-

nesses affirmed that other than grenades and bullets, the army used bazookas, particularly in Gonaïves. The army acted in uniform under the command of its officers: in Gonaïves Col. Gambetta Hippolyte directed the firing against the BED [Provincial Electoral Bureau.]"*

Another example of army involvement in the violence was provided by the observation team sent by the International Federation of the Rights of Man, a Paris-based non-governmental organization accredited to the United Nations. The team reported seeing the following incident at 117 Rue des Miracles in Port-au-Prince on November 29:

> "The crowd of voters had just been dispersed by shots from a car. While someone was explaining to us what had happened the same car returned and we heard gunshots; we all had to take shelter. Right next to us, a large military truck made no move. Sixteen soldiers occupied the back of the vehicle: they had seen everything without doing anything. They didn't intervene until it became evident that the people, exasperated, were going to go after the occupants of the car; they then interposed themselves between the people and the Macoutes, to protect the latter and escort them. We saw a person dressed in a military uniform on the back seat of the Macoute vehicle."

At 9:05 a.m. the CEP was forced to announce the postponement of the elections, and most of the nine electoral council members went into hiding. In a telephone call from his hiding place, CEP President Ernst Mirville described electoral officials as "walking dead men."

That afternoon, in flagrant violation of the Constitution, the CNG dissolved the CEP, claiming that the independent council had put itself above the law and allowed itself to be influenced by foreign powers. The military government had accomplished its goal: there would be no free elections.

---

* An official inquiry described "unidentified individuals" taking shelter in the Petite Riviere presbytery and, from it, opening fire on the army barracks next door. A recent visit to the site, however, showed that the church building was scarred by bullet holes while the barracks walls were smooth and apparently untouched. Haiti Information Libre, No. 34, August 1988, p. 11.

The violence had been so shocking that the US government, which up to then had refrained from condemning the military government or threatening to cut off aid, was finally moved to act. The Reagan administration announced the suspension of most military and economic aid to the Haitian government. Approximately $60 million in such aid planned for fiscal year 1988 was blocked but some $26 million in humanitarian aid, channeled through non-governmental organizations, was left in place.

D. The Substitute "Elections"

Dismayed at the cutoff in aid, the CNG quickly pledged to reschedule elections and set about organizing voting that it could control. From the start, the substitute elections of January 17, 1988 bore little resemblance to the earlier interrupted ones. All pretense of independence was removed from the new CNG-appointed electoral council when, before the members were even named, the CNG announced the date of the election. The new election law barred candidates, journalists and independent observers from polling places, but allowed the army to be present and to inspect voters' ballots. Much of the burden for printing and distributing ballots fell on the candidates themselves; since votes could not be cast for a candidate whose ballots had not arrived at the polling place, the candidates most favored by this abdication of responsibility for ballot distribution were those with access to the nation's best equipped distribution network -- the army. The military-dominated Supreme Court was permitted to review any CEP decision to bar former Duvalierist candidates. And anyone who "mistakenly" urged people not to vote could be fined and jailed.

Faced with this electoral charade, the four leading presidential candidates from the aborted November election -- Marc Bazin, Sylvio Claude, Louis Déjoie II and Gerard Gourgue -- who together accounted for over 80 percent of the anticipated November vote, announced that they would boycott the proposed substitute elections. The Haitian people widely followed their example.

The turnout for the January "contest" was generously estimated at no more than 10 percent. There were widespread reports of irregularities and fraud, including multiple voting, voting by minors and the purchasing of votes.

19

For example, our representatives, who visited 44 polling stations, saw polling places in Turgeau and Bois Verna where fewer than five persons had voted by 1:00 p.m. Five of the six largest polls in the capital never opened their doors. At other polling places, we spoke with 14- and 15-year-old youths who admitted having voted three or four times. At a site in Cité Soleil, Port-au-Prince's poorest slum, people were seen voting and then getting into a bus to drive to the Hotel de Ville to vote again. The drivers of some of these buses told us that Franck Romain, who would be named the "victor" of the Port-au-Prince mayoral election held the same day, had paid them to transport people to vote. Some of the youths said they were being paid one or two dollars for each time they voted. At some polling places, voters were permitted to vote more than once -- but always for the army's preferred candidate, Leslie Manigat. Their biggest problem was cleaning off the indelible ink into which voters were required to dip a fingertip.

The CNG made a two-pronged effort to legitimize the January 17 elections. First, on January 9, the military-controlled electoral council invoked Article 291 of the Constitution to reject eight presidential candidates as former Duvalierists. Second, the CNG picked as its "victor" Leslie Manigat, a professor who had earned a certain credibility during his many years in exile from the Duvalier dictatorship.

Why did the Namphy government bother? It seems clear that the strong international reaction to the November 29 massacre, the suspension of substantial quantities of international assistance, and the threats emanating from the US of a possible trade boycott or even military intervention had an effect on Haiti's rulers. Gen. Namphy hoped that by keeping the Duvalierist forces in the background and electing someone like Manigat, he could overcome international revulsion to the military regime and bring about the reestablishment of at least some aid.

The Duvalierists went along quietly with these moves. Unlike November 1987, there was no uproar when their candidates were stricken from the lists and no apparent disagreement with the Manigat choice. For all apparent purposes the army and the Duvalierists were united in their approach to the substitute elections: having prevented a true reformer and democrat from being

20

elected on November 29, they were willing to compromise and place a democratic figurehead in the presidency.

Despite certain anti-Duvalierist credentials, Manigat, as soon as he agreed to go along with the military's choice, was essentially a kept man. "Even if Manigat would like to permit certain liberties, certain political space," said Serge Gilles of the National Front for Concerted Action *(Front National de Concertation)* (FNC), "it will be hard for him. Manigat will be the prisoner of a Duvalierist Parliament, a Duvalierist Prime Minister and a Duvalierist army."

For unexplained reasons, the military-dominated electoral council did not announce the election verdict until a full week after January 17. Leslie Manigat was reported the winner with 50.38 percent of the vote, conveniently surpassing the 50 percent majority needed under the Constitution to avoid a runoff. The electoral council claimed that some 35 percent of Haiti's roughly 3 million voters had cast ballots, far above independent estimates.

E. Electoral Developments Under the Avril Government

Following the overthrow of the Manigat government in June 1988 and the ouster of the successor Namphy government in September 1988, Lt. Gen. Prosper Avril, a key behind-the-scenes actor in the previous governments, assumed the presidency. In early November 1988, the Avril government, under pressure from all sides to show some movement toward democracy, proposed the creation of an Electoral College of Haiti *(Collège Electoral d'Haïti)* (CEDHA), which was to have been under the jurisdiction of the Ministry of Justice. The proposed body would not have been independent, and its members would have been subject to military influence.

As noted, the Haitian Constitution of 1987 called for elections to be managed by an electoral council, the CEP, which operated independently of the government. That independence was in large part guaranteed by the fact that each of nine members of the CEP was designated by a different sector of Haitian society (the Catholic Church, human rights groups, the Supreme Court, etc.). The electoral college initially proposed by the Avril government, by functioning under Justice Ministry supervision, would have lacked this crucial independence. Moreover, the nine members of what would have been designated an Electoral Council within the college, instead of representing different sectors of society, would have been chosen from the nine geographical departments of the country and appointed by "decree of the Executive Power," an invitation to military influence.

The response to this proposal from political parties and human rights groups was highly critical, with most groups rejecting the lack of independence of the proposed college and underscoring the need for urgent measures to improve security before elections could be considered. The Committee for Democratic Unity *(Comité d'Entente Democratique)* (CED), representing at the time three of the leading presidential candidates in the aborted November 1987 elections, replied: "The Constitution of 1987 must be an indispensable reference.... The absolute independence of the Electoral Council is a condition of its credibility and hence its effectiveness..., independence ... not only with regard to the government but also with regard to political parties and groups."

KONAKOM, the National Committee of the Congress of Democratic Movements *(Comité National du Congrés des Mouvements Démocratiques)* said: "It is inappropriate to launch moves toward the electoral process without setting in motion a series of effective measures of security and justice, indispensable conditions capable of restoring the confidence of the citizens and encouraging them to participate seriously" in the elections. This coalition of several hundred mass-based groups suggested that the government work with the different political sectors in the country to develop a plan for an electoral council that was independent and that would be granted all the necessary financial and logistical support, as well as security, necessary for its functioning.

The National Agricultural and Industrial Party *(Parti Agricole et Industriel National)* (PAIN) of Louis Déjoie described the proposal as unconstitutional and called for a "return to the Constitution of 1987, with the exception of arrangements contrary to the nature of the *de facto* provisional government ... [as well as] disarming of paramilitary forces and judging the authors of the crimes committed November 29, 1987 and September 11, 1988."

Three months after it was issued, Gen. Avril's proposal for an electoral commission was debated in a forum with representatives of some 28 political, labor and professional groups. These included the Movement to Establish

Democracy in Haiti *(Mouvement pour l'Instauration de la Démocratie en Haïti)* (MIDH), the National Progressive Revolutionary Haitian Party *(Parti National Progressiste Revolutionnaire Haïtien)* (PANPRHA), the Unified Haitian Communist Party (PUCH), the 28th of November National Patriotic Movement *(Mouvement Patriotique National du 28 Novembre)* (MNP 28), the Independent Federation of Haitian Workers affiliated with the Confederation of Latin American Workers (CATH-CLAT), The Federation of Unionized Workers *(Federation des Ouvriers Syndiqués)* (FOS) and several very minor groups. Participants also included former Duvalier government officials and a political figure associated with Gen. Namphy's government, Gregoire Eugene, who was named special advisor to the president after Gen. Namphy ousted Leslie Manigat on June 19-20, 1988.

A large number of democratic groups boycotted the forum because of the mounting repression of the Avril government, detailed in Chapter IV. Among them were KONAKOM; the Independent Federation of Haitian Workers *(Centrale Autonome des Travailleurs Haïtiens)* (CATH), the largest and most politically active trade union in Haiti; the Haitian Christian Democratic Party (PDCH); PAIN; and the Papaye Peasant Movement *(Mouvement Paysan de Papaye)* (MPP), Haiti's largest peasant organization.

The forum, held on February 9 to 17, 1989, recommended the establishment of an independent electoral council to run the elections which closely paralleled the original CEP established under Article 289 of the Constitution. The proposed council would be composed of nine representatives from nine different sectors of Haitian society, e.g., human rights groups, the journalists' association, the Catholic Church, labor unions, including one seat for the military government. On February 23, 1989, the Avril government accepted this proposal, although it has yet to be implemented as this report goes to press, and no date for elections has been set. Nor have such crucial issues been addressed as the manner in which the independence of the council would be guaranteed or the status of Article 291 of the still-suspended Haitian Constitution, which, as noted, bars from public office for ten years architects of the Duvalier dictatorship as well as those who embezzled public funds or engaged in political assassination or torture. Most important, as detailed in the remainder of this report, the Avril government has yet to halt the ongoing political violence and intimidation which threaten any future elections. To the contrary, at the same time as he accepted the proposed council, Gen. Avril appointed Col. Acédius Saint-Louis, an officer with a long established and apparently cultivated image of brutality, to the top security post of Defense and Interior Minister, replacing the more moderate Col. Carl Dorsainvil.

F. Requirements for Free and Fair Elections

In our view, quite apart from the body that will organize elections, several steps are necessary to guarantee reasonably fair and free elections in Haiti. First and foremost, the electoral process must be made free of violence and the fear of violence. The acting government must exercise control over the army, disarm paramilitary forces, and assure that voter registration, voter education, campaigning and voting take place in a secure atmosphere in which people can vote without fear of reprisal. The armed forces must act swiftly and within the law against brutality or intimidation from any quarter, including its own ranks. The government must make its opposition to rule by terror public, firm and unyielding.

As part of this effort, the rule of law must be established. That means that all sectors of society, including the military, must be subject to the law as applied by independent judicial tribunals. An important starting point would be ensuring that the authors of past violent crimes -- such as the killings of November 1987 and the September 1988 massacre in St. Jean Bosco church, as well as the terror of the Duvalier decades -- be sought out, prosecuted and tried openly by an independent judiciary.

Second, basic freedoms of speech, association and assembly must be assured. A fair election can take place only when candidates and the electorate are free to speak and organize without endangering themselves or their families. The media, including radio and television, must be permitted freely to cover the campaign and the issues, presenting the candidates and their views to a wide public. Haitians everywhere must feel free to form political parties, labor unions and other civic organizations, which in turn must be free to take part in the election. Only then will all adults be able to make an informed choice, based on reasonably complete information about the issues and the views of various candidates.

Finally, as the democratic forum has proposed and the Avril government apparently has accepted, an independent, nonpartisan authority, such as the CEP envisioned in the March 1987 Constitution, must be in charge of organizing, carrying out and tallying the vote. This group must be free to carry out its mandate without threats or intimidations, and with adequate funding and active assistance from the acting government on both logistical and security matters.

III. POLITICAL VIOLENCE AND INTIMIDATION

A. Overview

While the violent crushing of the November 1987 elections was the most visible indication that military and paramilitary forces were willing to resort to violence rather than relinquish power to civilian democrats, it, unfortunately, has not been the only such indication. Just as the crushed elections were preceded by a summer and fall of often murderous attacks on demonstrators and participants in the electoral process, so the following fifteen months have been marked by repeated outbursts of officially sponsored and officially sanctioned violence. This violence has occurred under each of the governments of the last fifteen months, including the current government of Lt. Gen. Prosper Avril.

The intensity of the violence has varied, generally with the degree to which ruling forces perceive their hold on power threatened. At times there has been relatively little, as in the months immediately following the November 1987 elections, when the Haitian population remained cowed by the ruthless display of force on election day. Other times violence has intensified, due either to turmoil within the military, as during the "insecurity" of April and May 1988, or to increasingly assertive, though nonviolent, popular opposition to military rule, as during the summer of 1988. As this report goes to press, both factors appear to be contributing to persistent and possibly accelerating political violence.

Much of this military and paramilitary violence was directed against those exercising their freedom of assembly and association. Frequent victims were members of the *Ti Legliz* (religious base communities, or "Little Church") and other progressive segments of the church; peasant organizations such as the MPP and labor organizations affiliated with CATH. These groups were targeted both because they had led the resistance to the old order under Duvalier and because they have continued at the forefront of opposition to the military-dominated governments that succeeded the Duvalier dictatorship. In certain cases outspoken critics of the government were also the focus of abuses. And in a significant number of cases, apparently random citizens were victimized.

As during the election day massacre of November 1987, paramilitary forces were on the front line of much of the violence. These forces often were composed in substantial part of the remnants of the dreaded Tontons Macoutes. Although the Macoutes, known officially as the Volunteers for National Security *(Volontaires de la Sécurité Nationale)* (VSN), were formally disbanded following the departure of Duvalier, many VSN personnel were absorbed by the military as attachés affiliated with such posts as the Dessalines Barracks (Casernes Dessalines) and *Recherches Criminelles.* As attachés, these plainclothes military adjuncts were armed, authorized to carry weapons, and given effective license to use deadly force. Other VSN personnel continued to operate without known formal military affiliation, under such burgeoning paramilitary organizations as the *Sans Mamans,* literally, the "Motherless Ones." They were aided by the military's token efforts to disarm the Macoutes following their formal dissolution, an effort which, by reliable estimates, left several thousand weapons in private hands.

These paramilitary forces operated with considerable support from the army, usually tacit but at times active. Uniformed soldiers frequently accompanied irregular forces as they engaged in acts of political violence, either directing the violence or playing an important back-up role. Even when army troops were not on the scene, their consistent failure to bring perpetrators to justice gave a green light to further violence in defense of the established order.

These patterns have not been altered by the current government of Gen. Avril. No prosecutorial effort has been made to curtail the activities of the *Sans Mamans* and other paramilitary troops. Nor has there been any public effort to rein in the attachés. Largely as a result of pressure from the army rank and file, the Avril government in its first month in power conducted several well-publicized raids of paramilitary arsenals. But few weapons were recovered and these efforts ceased after some of the junior officers and soldiers who pushed for them were jailed. Violent attacks thus have continued, at times with the participation of uniformed troops.

As a result, three years after the downfall of Jean-Claude Duvalier, the political violence that characterized the Duvalier dictatorship has become a disturbingly regular feature of the Haitian landscape. A cessation of that violence, and the disarming of the irregular forces that are immediately responsible for much of it, is a necessary condition of any move toward elected, civilian rule. The Avril government has made painfully little progress in this regard.

B. The National Governing Council

The killings and brazen violence did not end with the collapse of the November 1987 elections. There were other outbursts of violence over the next two months as the CNG sought to compel the Haitian population to accept its plan for substitute, military-controlled elections. On December 21, at a memorial service for the victims of the November 29 massacre held at the Basilica Notre Dame, three gunmen fired at protesters leaving the service. One man, Merovée Ideli, was killed, and at least three others, including Jean-Claude Christophe and Jean-Claude Salomon, were wounded. According to some witnesses, the gunmen were wearing police and army uniforms and arrived in a military truck.

On January 8, 1988, according to Radio Métropole, the police in the southern town of Cayes-Jacmel arrested and held overnight "many people" for political activity in connection with an unnamed presidential candidate. Three days later, Radio Métropole also reported that squads of soldiers in the southwestern town of Jérémie were rounding up those advocating a boycott of the scheduled January 17 elections. Two of those arrested, according to the League of Former Political Prisoners *(Ligue des Anciens Prisonniers Politique Haïtiens)* (LAPPH), were Michel Mébreu and Mario Dominique.

In the period between the January 17 electoral charade and the inauguration of Leslie Manigat as president on February 7, 1988, Haitians sought peaceful ways of protesting the sham electoral event that had led to Manigat's selection by the army. Scores of people faced official reprisals for circulating a petition challenging the elections. Among them, according to Radio Soleil, were those actively soliciting signatures on behalf of the FNC. For example, on January 28, Sgt. Leconte Christopher detained and beat Jean Herold Casimir, a local coordinator for the FNC in Mirebalais in the Artibonite valley, for collecting petition signatures.

Similarly, Radio Soleil reported on February 2, 1988 that several peasants who had signed this petition in the Central Plateau were being harassed by local authorities. One priest, Father Estimé, rector of the local parish of La Victoire in the Central Plateau, was arrested on January 31 by the local army commander, Gabriel Pinasse, while conducting a service in which he informed his parishioners of the petition drive; he was released only after local residents demonstrated in his favor in front of the police station. In addition, residents of La Gonâve, the island in the bay of Port-au-Prince, complained in an interview broadcast by Radio Haïti-Inter that the local section chief had detained and beaten them for denouncing the January 17 elections; they complained that several peasants had been forced into hiding and that at least one had been arrested.

On January 20, Louis Déjoie II, one of the four major presidential candidates of the November 1987 elections and the head of PAIN, was arrested upon returning from a trip abroad in which he had lobbied against recognizing the legitimacy of the January 17 elections. After being held for four hours without explanation at the airport, he was taken in handcuffs by plainclothes police officers and shoved into a waiting pick-up truck. When he attempted to speak with concerned supporters, he was slapped across the face by a police officer. The arresting officers were accompanied by troops from the Casernes Dessalines. Déjoie was released two days later, after considerable domestic and international pressure.

The same day as Déjoie's release, Dr. Louis Roy, the principal architect of the Haitian Constitution, was detained without charge at the Port-au-Prince airport as he arrived from Canada. He was released 2-1/2 hours later after having been warned about statements he made while abroad that were critical of the military-run elections.

Organized peasant movements were frequently the victims of violence and intimidation efforts under the CNG. In January, at least 16 members of the Small Peasants' Collective of St. Suzanne *(Collectif pour l'Avancement des Petits Paysans Haïtiens)* were arrested by local authorities; pleas for their release went unanswered until their situation became public on February 27, when members of the organization denounced the illegality of their continued detention.

Members of the MPP, which operates in the Central Plateau region, were branded subversives by local authorities, particularly Maj. Serges David and Lt. Gabriel Pinasse, and several had their huts ransacked. At least eleven MPP members were detained for several hours on January 13, 1988. According to the local priest, Father Gabriel Bien-Aimé, many were intimidated and forced to flee the area for several weeks following the January 17 "elections," including literacy workers, members of the *Ti Legliz*, and at least two physicians, Drs. Henrys and Barbot, who ran a community clinic in Thomonde.

The Artibonite valley, the scene of several violent land disputes and a "rice war" in 1987, remained volatile into 1988. On January 26, 1988, a military raid in "Lachicote" left a number of peasants wounded by bullets or beatings and produced several arrests. Several huts were also set on fire. The raid stemmed from a dispute between peasants and Salim Athie, one of Haiti's largest landlords. Athie had gained a reputation during the 1970's for having acquired most of what now constitutes his property in the valley through the forced expropriation of peasant land. This violent takeover of the land was facilitated by Athie's close ties to officials of the Duvalier regime, on whom he bestowed large favors, including gifts of portions of the land he illegally acquired.

C. The Manigat Government

The advent of a civilian president, Leslie Manigat, did little to reduce the use of political violence. Manigat's lack of impact on the military's use of force for political purposes reflected his dependence on that institution for having selected him, in patently fraudulent elections, to be its civilian face.

On March 25, 1988, military authorities forcibly dispersed a peaceful demonstration by inhabitants of Gonaïves to protest the illegal dumping of allegedly toxic waste on the shores of this city; the dumping of the toxic waste had been authorized by then Commerce Minister Mario Celestin, and the fee for permitting such dumping was widely believed to have been pocketed by Col. Jean-Claude Paul and government associates. On March 29, local troops in the

31

northwestern town of Beauchamps dispersed a meeting of 40 peasants organized to celebrate the first anniversary of the popularly enacted Constitution; all the participants were arrested without charge and placed in detention for 24 hours. Similarly, on April 4, military authorities broke up a peaceful demonstration in the town of Petit-Goave in southern Haiti, which was held to protest the illegitimacy of Manigat's regime and to demand new national and local elections. And on May 3, in Port-au-Prince, a demonstration held by workers at Chancerelles Manufacturing was broken up by the police, and several demonstrators were severely beaten.

The offices and homes of several political figures in Port-au-Prince were subjected to searches that appeared to be politically motivated. On March 22, 1987, armed men entered the home of Turneb Delpe, a leading member of the National Progressive Democratic Party of Haiti *(Parti National Democratique Progressiste Haïtien)* (PNDPH), and seized Party documents. On March 24, soldiers searched the headquarters of the United Front for the Liberation of Haiti *(Front Uni de Liberation Nationale d'Haiti)*(FULNH) and confiscated all documents written on the organization's letterhead. And on March 25, troops from the Casernes Dessalines searched the Champs de Mars Pharmacy, owned by Gladys Lauture, a leading member of the Brotherhood of Progressive Religious Workers *(Fraternité des Laïques Engagés)* and a strong supporter of the CEP.

Catholic priests identified with the *Ti Legliz* movement increasingly became the targets of attacks. On June 3, in Fond Verrettes, the presbytery and the dispensary were shot at. On June 4, 1988, unidentified individuals fired gunshots at a church in Cayes-Jacmel, forcing Father Lorisme, several nuns and the entire Saint-Theresa congregation to flee for their lives; the later discovery at the scene of a bottle filled with gasoline, matches and some firewood led observers to conclude that the attack was a failed arson attempt.

Human rights monitors were also targeted. On May 21, 1988, Daniel O'Bastiani was arrested by military authorities. O'Bastiani, acting on behalf of the Ecumenical Center for Human Rights *(Centre Oecuménique des Droits de l'Homme)*, had served as a guide in the Central Plateau for two representatives of the New York-based Lawyers Committee for Human Rights. O'Bastiani was taken to the military barracks in Gonaïves where he was beaten and accused of "bringing shame" to the country through his assistance of the Lawyers Committee representatives. An attorney for the Ecumenical Center obtained O'Bastiani's release after visiting the barracks commander.

Similarly, at the end of May or the beginning of June 1988, the police visited the **Karl Leveque Center** *(Centre Karl Leveque)* in downtown Port-au-Prince, a human rights organization which addresses the plight of Haitians who return to Haiti from the Bahamas and the Dominican Republic. Claiming that the Center was harboring a person accused of subversive activities, the police entered the premises without a warrant and threatened employees and the director, Paul Dejean.

A particularly striking episode of official violence occurred on May 28, 1988, when troops went on a rampage in an area known as Danti, in the Artibonite valley. According to witnesses, the troops carried automatic weapons, grenades, gasoline and tear gas. They burned down at least 110 huts, beat and arrested some peasants, and took off with the peasants' livestock, including goats, chickens, cows and wild turkeys. The victims explained the rampage as the result of the refusal of local authorities to implement an August 1986 order of the Justice Ministry, which, at the insistence of the local population, had reversed an earlier decision of the Duvalier government to transfer Danti from the district of Gros Morne to that of Borgnes. The military authorities were believed to have resorted to the extreme violence in May 1988 because the villagers had insisted on having the August 1986 order implemented.

Much of the violence during the four months of the Manigat presidency was directed against seemingly random targets. Referred to by Haitians as the "insecurity," this violence, most pronounced in April and May, left bodies on the streets of Port-au-Prince on a regular basis, sowing terror among the citizenry. According to LAPPH, 17 were killed from bullet wounds in and around Port-au-Prince between April 15 and May 4, 1988. Most of the victims either were never identified or were uninvolved in politics.

Although it was difficult to determine who was responsible for these killings, or their purpose, most observers attributed them to an attempt by Gen. Namphy, at the time armed forces commander-in-chief, as well as those allied with him, to destabilize the Manigat government and provide a pretext for Namphy's return as head of state. Indeed, reliable reports indicated that a group of army soldiers loyal to Gen. Namphy shed their uniforms and operated as a death squad in Port-au-Prince. Reportedly, this group of soldiers was arrested by troops of the Casernes Dessalines. Col. Jean-Claude Paul, then the commander of the Dessalines Battalion, was said to have been motivated to make the arrests because he had allied himself with Manigat, in part for support in avoiding extradition to face charges of narcotics trafficking then pending against him in Miami. The arrests prompted Namphy to attempt to dismiss Paul; Manigat, in turn, attempted to dismiss Namphy and remove many of Namphy's high-ranking military allies; Manigat then found himself overthrown by forces loyal to Namphy, who assumed the presidency.

D. The Namphy Government

Buttressing the belief that much of the "insecurity" under the Manigat government had been the work of forces allied with Gen. Namphy, these seemingly random murders quickly subsided following the coup of June 19-20, 1988, which returned Gen. Namphy to the head of government. Violence of a more directed sort continued, however. Many of its victims were those seeking to organize the peasantry. The violence was most acute in the countryside, where approximately 80% of Haiti's population lives.

1. The Countryside

a. The Closing of Offices of The Federation of Agricultural Workers

During our visit to Haiti in August 1988, we interviewed representatives of two branches of the Federation of Agricultural Workers *(Fédération des Travailleurs Agricoles)*, a CATH affiliate, which had recently been the subject of violent attacks. They reported:

> The Federation attempted to open an office in Gros Morne on July 25, 1988. That night, at about midnight, automatic weapon fire was sprayed at the office. Although the office was located about 15 or 20 meters from the local police station, no official intervened. The local authorities had accused CATH

34

of being a communist organization which only pretends to help the peasants. Three days later, on July 28, the local authorities in an open meeting announced to the nine rural section chiefs of Gros Morne and other assembled Macoutes and soldiers that they were not to allow any meetings to take place without prior authorization. On August 4, that message was reaffirmed by the district military commander.

The Federation office in St. Michel de l'Attalaye suffered a similar fate. The office opened on June 26, 1988. On the night of June 27, the military ransacked and destroyed the office. They seized equipment and other material, then went to the cemetery and burned it. Although the brick building housing the offices was not destroyed, five wooden doors were removed and burned. When the Federation members reported the attack to the local magistrate, a woman named "Levallat," and to the local lieutenant, a man named "Jules," they were told that the destruction of the office could have been avoided if they had received authorization to establish the office. They were told that they needed authorization to function. When, on August 3, a representative from the Federation office in St. Michel de l'Attalaye was preparing to come to Port-au-Prince to report the incident, a member of the local communal section assembly (CASEC) confronted him and in an aggressive manner asked about his intentions, his departure date, and his anticipated route.

b. The Murder of Four Members of the Labadie Youth Movement

As the summer progressed, abuses in the countryside became more violent and deadly. On August 14, 1988, members of the Labadie Youth Movement (Mouvement des Jeunes de Labadie) (MJL), a peasant youth organization based in Labadie in the Artibonite, held a meeting to celebrate the second anniversary of their founding. According to Radio Haïti-Inter and Radio Antilles Internationale, a few minutes after the meeting ended a group of assailants, led by the town's prefect, Baguidy Grand Pierre, and the local section chief, Espérance Charles, opened fire and killed four participants: Berson Etienne, Doni Accéus, Armand Louismond and Alex Alexandre. At least ten others were wounded. The next day, a combined military-civilian commission sent by the

35

Namphy government organized a meeting reportedly to investigate the attack. According to the MJL, the commission included the two government officials who had participated in the killings of the day before. Predictably, it blamed the MJL for the incident and claimed that the organization was communist-led. Since its creation, the MJL has called for land reform and for an end to over-charging by collectors of market taxes. The August 14 killings crowned a long list of arbitrary arrests and threats against MJL members.

c. The Arrest and Beating of Eight Members of the Papaye Peasant Movement

Five days later, on August 19, eight members of the MPP were arrested in Abriyo, a small settlement in the mountains near Hinche in the Central Plateau. Those arrested were Elius Absalon, Rozan Deris, Lenoit Elisma, Louima Ferile, Denis François, Letoit François, Delius Saint-Hilaire and Edouane Saintina. The MPP has been a forceful advocate for small farmers' and peasants' rights. The eight MPP members were taken the following day, August 20, to the office of Maj. Serge David, commander of the Central Military Department. As they were being interrogated by Maj. David, they were hit repeatedly -- often with cupped hands over the ears -- by soldiers standing behind them, and they were threatened with death if they did not leave the MPP. Saintina, who was identified as the leader of the eight, was subjected to particularly brutal treatment. Maj. David himself pulled and tore the beard of one peasant, who fainted. The eight were released on August 22, after being charged with refusing to pay market taxes. The same day, they were examined by a doctor who found the following:

1. Edoane Saintina

-- Perforation of two eardrums; emission of blood and clear liquid from both ears.

-- Bilateral conjunctiva ecchymosis (bruises to the membrane which lines the eyelid).

-- Hematoma (swelling caused by loose blood under the skin) on his buttocks.

2. Rozan Deris

-- Perforation of the right eardrum.

-- Conjunctiva ecchymosis.

3. Elius Absalon

-- Conjunctiva ecchymosis.

-- Hematoma on his buttocks.

4. Denis François

-- Hematoma on the lower jaw.

5. Lenoit Elisma

-- Conjunctiva ecchymosis.

6. Louima Ferile

-- Conjunctiva ecchymosis.

7. Letoit François

-- Strong headaches and pains in the jaw.

8. Delius Saint-Hilaire

-- Trauma of the left wrist consistent with a fracture of the radius (the bone in the forearm on the thumb side), secondary to a blow from a baton.

-- Conjunctiva ecchymosis.

Also on August 20, MPP leader Chavannes Jean-Baptiste was arrested at his home in Papaye, outside Hinche, and detained in the army barracks for five hours. Charges of inciting subversion were later dropped.

d. Other Violence and Arrests

Other violence and arrests directed against peasant activities in the countryside, according to LAPPH and the Haitian Center for Human Rights *(Centre Haïtien de Defense des Libertés Publiques)* (CHADEL), included the following:

- On August 3, approximately 12 peasants in Cayes-Jacmel were detained, mistreated and accused of being communists.

- On August 5, in Les Cayes, Sergo Joseph was arrested and severely beaten for writing anti-government slogans on walls during a tour of the region by Gen. Namphy. He was hospitalized for nearly two months in Les Cayes under military guard before being freed following the September 17 coup.

- On August 6, after a meeting of the planters' union of Bayonais in the Artibonite, two union leaders, Levelt Saint Louis and Toussaint Saint Louis, were arrested and sent to prison in Gonaïves.

- On August 11, in Verrettes in the Artibonite, a paramilitary force set fire to a peasant grain warehouse. According to the victims, the arsonists vowed to set fire to all premises used by the *Ti Legliz* to hold meetings.

- On August 16, in Bossou, a rural community near La Chapelle in the Artibonite, a group of armed men led by the town's mayor opened fire to disperse approximately 150 young people who had gathered in the Catholic church to discuss the political situation. The assailants arrested three participants in the meeting because it had been held without prior authorization from the army.

e. The Expulsion of Father René Poirier

The case of Father René Poirier, a 54-year-old Canadian priest stationed in Grand Goave in southern Haiti, illustrates the pressures placed on those seeking to organize or assemble the peasantry. On August 5, the government announced that it had arrested and expelled Father Poirier because he had made "public and insulting statements of a nature to compromise the political and social order of the country." The government never clarified the nature of Father Poirier's "insulting statements," but it was widely believed that he was expelled for refusing an invitation to welcome Gen. Namphy as he passed through Grand Goave.

The expulsion came at a time when the Namphy government, in power for less than two months, had begun to take the offensive in seeking to establish its legitimacy. Two weeks earlier, Gen. Namphy had announced, with great fanfare, the launching of various "microprojects" *(microprojets)* -- small water systems and other such development projects -- and had taken to the road in an attempt to demonstrate popular backing. According to an August 6 press advisory from the Information Ministry, everywhere Namphy went he was hailed as a "symbol of courage" and a "champion of democracy." Father Poirier's "offense" seems to have been his public refusal to share this view.

Father Poirier also offered a possible alternative explanation for his expulsion: a long standing dispute with the rural section chief of St. Anne, known as Danger. The conflict began when Danger insisted on knowing the identities of those who attended services in the chapel, as well as what Father Poirier said during those services. Replying that he did not make that kind of a report even to his superiors, Father Poirier asked the section chief whether he was a Macoute. Danger replied that he was baptized a Christian, to which Father Poirier retorted: "Duvalier, too, was baptized."

On August 9, in reaction to the expulsion, about 500 supporters of Father Poirier organized a vigil at the presbytery of Grand Goave. At 2 a.m., the army appeared, fired several shots in the air, and arrested five youths who were guarding the entrance to the presbytery: Frantz Pascal, Narélien Normil, Frantz Belrus, Kerline Belrus and Berrouet Lafontant. Three of the youths were released on August 10. The other two, Pascal and Normil, were brought initially before a judge in Grand Goave, who said the case was beyond his competence, and then to the military barracks in Petit Goave. They were released a few days later after extensive public protest. Father Poirier ultimately was permitted to return to Haiti on October 9.

2. Port-au-Prince

Although violence under Gen. Namphy was most pervasive in the countryside, Port-au-Prince was not immune. The severity of the incidents accelerated with time, ultimately leading to a bloody massacre that paved the way for the overthrow of the Namphy government.

a. The Ransacking of the Home of Laennec Hurbon

On July 3, in Musseau, four men armed with Uzis and walkie-talkies searched and ransacked the home of Laennec Hurbon. An ex-priest turned researcher and writer, Hurbon reportedly had been collecting information on the aborted elections of November 29, 1987.

39

b. The Murder of Lafontant Joseph

On July 11, the body of Lafontant Joseph, a 54-year-old human rights attorney, was found in his jeep on a small street off the road to the international airport outside Port-au-Prince. The body was badly mutilated, one ear was missing and the tongue had been partially cut off. There was a deep gash going from the oesophagus to the liver which seemed to have been made by a bayonet or similar sword. There was also a single gunshot wound.

Joseph had a long history of defending human rights. As an attorney, he specialized in representing trade unions. He was one of the founders of the Haitian League for Human Rights *(Ligue Haitienne des Droits Humains)* and was Executive Secretary of the Center for the Promotion of Human Rights *(Centre de Promotion des Droits Humains)*. He had also been a candidate for the senate in the aborted November 29 elections, running as a representative of the FNC. Like most other candidates, he refused to participate in the substitute elections of January 17, 1988. He had been imprisoned twice under Jean-Claude Duvalier.

In the week before his death, Joseph received an anonymous telephone call from someone threatening to kill him and to kidnap his seven-year-old son. Joseph communicated this threat to Radio Soleil and Radio Haïti-Inter. Two days before his death, he received another anonymous telephone call warning him that he would be killed the following Sunday. Again, Joseph informed the two radio stations. Joseph was killed sometime early the next Monday morning.

On the eve of his death, Joseph was last seen by his family at approximately 7:00 p.m. Joseph and three companions (two men and a woman) reportedly were seen at a bar near Joseph's home at around midnight, as the four left the bar. As detailed in Chapter VI, the government's investigation of the Joseph killing has been far from satisfactory.

Joseph's funeral, scheduled for July 16, 1988 at Sacre Coeur church, was canceled when the church received threats from unidentified telephone callers. The family was forced to proceed directly to the cemetery. The memorial mass was said a few days later by Father Jean-Bertrand Aristide before approximately 1,000 mourners.

c. Other Killings

As the summer wore on, seemingly random killings resumed, as the government appeared to promote or countenance violence as a tool for quelling an increasingly restive populace. Most of the killings were by unidentified gunmen. According to LAPPH and CHADEL:

- On July 13, the decapitated body of a 35-year-old unidentified man was found on the outskirts of Port-au-Prince.

- On July 14, in Morne-a-Cabrit, northwest of Port-au-Prince on the road to Mirebalais, the body of an unidentified young woman was found in a pool of blood.

- On July 25, armed men opened fire from a car on a group of people in Delmas, part of metropolitan Port-au-Prince, wounding two: Jean-Claude François and a man identified only as Pierre.

- On July 26, the body of an unidentified young man was found riddled with bullets on Ruelle Canne-à-Sucre in Carrefour, a section of Port-au-Prince.

- On August 2, the body of an unidentified young man was found riddled with bullets in Delmas.

- On August 17, an unidentified man in his twenties was shot by a detective belonging to *Recherches Criminelles*. The detectives had tried to arrest the man but he had refused by lying down on the pavement, near the office of the national telephone company (Teleco) in downtown Port-au-Prince. One of the detectives then pulled out his gun and shot the man to death in full view of several witnesses.

- On August 24, Jean Bodouin, a truck driver, was found dead at the Bicentenaire in downtown Port-au-Prince.

- On September 4, a traffic policeman shot Wickmy Malivert severely in the stomach because Malivert had not paid his traffic ticket.

- And on September 15, the body of an unidentified man was found at the corner of the Boulevard Jean-Jacques Dessalines and Rue Bonne Foi in downtown Port-au-Prince.

41

d. The Attack on the Church of St. Jean Bosco

The most brutal attack in Haiti since the aborted November 1987 elections occurred on September 11, 1988 in the La Saline section of Port-au-Prince. The target of the attack was the St. Jean Bosco church, where Father Jean-Bertrand Aristide, a charismatic populist priest, was saying mass.

Shortly after the start of the 9:00 a.m. mass, thugs armed with guns and wielding machetes stormed the church, killing 12 parishioners and wounding at least 77. The church was doused in gasoline and set ablaze. The perpetrators, believed to be former members of the Tontons Macoutes, committed these crimes while uniformed army soldiers watched nearby and even cordoned off the area, refusing to lend assistance to the victims or to intervene to stop the killings and shootings.

A few hours later, both the Catholic Church's Radio Soleil and the independent Radio Cacique were attacked by the marauding gangs. The offices of two political parties were also ransacked, as were two other churches, including the Immaculate Conception Church of Father Arthur Volel in Cité Soleil, known for the charitable role it plays in that slum. Witnesses to the killings in the church identified at least two members of the gang as deputies of Col. Franck Romain, then the Mayor of Port-au-Prince, who, in a public statement, justified the murderous actions as legitimate. The next day, five self-described members of the gang appeared on Radio Métropole and Télé Haïti to warn that the slaughter was mere "child's play" and to vow other attacks.

The following eyewitness testimony from a member of the church's youth corps was recorded the day after the massacre by a reliable informant:

> "The situation that evolved at St. Jean Bosco yesterday is a situation that has been unfolding since last Sunday [a week before the attack], or even earlier. Last Sunday, while Aristide was saying mass, this guy appeared, but the church's youth had been trying to assure the church's safety, and they suspected this guy who in fact was carrying a gun. Well, he tried to get through to the altar, but if you know St. Jean Bosco on a Sunday, there are a lot of people, a lot of them sitting on the floor, and it's hard to get through. The guy tried to push people aside so that he could pass, but the youths in charge of security

grabbed him, and he had a big gun on him, a .48. I don't know arms very well, but anyway they grabbed him and they took his .48, and he said to them "gimme my gun," but he saw that the kids had it, and he ran away. There was no press there to take his picture. He wasn't by himself. He was with two other guys, but when they saw that he had been caught, they fled. We hit the first guy a couple of times, and we kept his gun. He fled. We called the Justice of the Peace to tell him that we had this gun and we called the Papal Nuncio to come pick it up....

"On Tuesday evening, for Father Aristide's mass, we again established security methods, we monitored the people coming in.... Everything was tense. After the mass on Tuesday night, there were threats and a rumor that an attack was coming. The mass ended about seven, and people were leaving. Some of us young people were inside, and we stayed. And then at 7:15, or 7:20, there came rocks and the bullets started flying. Everyone inside ran for shelter; rocks and bullets kept coming, all night they kept throwing rocks and shooting at the church.

"So that was the situation and we announced this to the press. But all week there was a rumor that they were going to come kill people, that they were going to make another Jean-Rabel [a massacre during the summer of 1987 in the provincial town of Jean-Rabel in which at least 135 people were killed] at the church. We got phone calls daily telling us not to have the mass on Sunday; we knew we were facing danger.

"Sunday morning came, and we put our security plans into action, so that we could combat whatever was going to happen that morning.... Around eight o'clock, the faithful began to arrive for the nine o'clock mass. The church was full, as usual. We closed the big front gate as a security measure the minute Aristide entered the church. As the people came in, they were searched to make sure they did not carry weapons. So the mass began; Aristide appeared, he read from the Gospels, and he [unclear who] was in front of the gate with two other youths, because although we had ordered the gate closed, we needed someone there so that if people came late we could identify them and let them in. And then, ten minutes after the mass began, at about 9:15, they started throwing rocks again. Then, even though the gate was closed, they came and broke it down.

It is clear that these were Franck Romain's people, that they organized and planned the attack.

"Almost a hundred guys with machetes, spikes, knives and guns, they walked over, they shot at the church, and then they broke through the gates. It took them about five, ten minutes from the beginning of the attack to when they broke through the gates. I ran, some people who were in the church went into the back courtyard, but since I couldn't get through, I ran through the front courtyard over to the CORAN [the other church building inside the front courtyard, catty corner to the church], and I hid in a room from which I could watch the whole street [Grand Rue, or Boulevard Dessalines, Port-au-Prince's main street].

"I saw guys from the Haitian army, in olive green, with big trucks, accompanied by Franck Romain's men, the aggressors, and the army was covering them, giving them security while they were firing on the church. Meanwhile these guys went into the church, they beat people, they shot them, they killed them, and then some of them went and bought gasoline so that they could set the church on fire. The whole time, the army was protecting them, the "forces of order" had surrounded the church, on every side, on the street next to the Salésian Mother, on Delmas, everywhere, there were the police, and there were Franck Romain's men, all wearing red arm-bands. I saw Franck Romain with my own eyes, running the show outside. He was in a white car, talking to the guys, just before the whole thing began.

"So the shooting went on and on, people were dying. People were wounded, they burned down the church, they burned all the cars, almost all the cars in the courtyard, the cars of people who had come to hear a mass, they burned all their cars, they stole a car, they burned the car of a journalist who was there; these guys did a lot of damage.

"I must say that some of us tried to defend ourselves, because a few of them were injured too. When they finished burning the church, they tried to get into the inner courtyard, but we fought them off with rocks. So they couldn't get in where so many of the faithful were hiding.

44

"The attack lasted two or three hours, from about nine until about 11:30. Just before noon, they began to leave, the situation seemed calm. But there was still some shooting, and this guy who had lost his red armband during the melee, he tried to come in, acting like he wasn't one of them. But we recognized him and we grabbed him, and that was when the police came in, finally.

"Father Mésidor [the head of the Salésians, who arrived about that time on the scene] asked us to open the gate [to the inner courtyard], so we went to find the key for him, but meanwhile, some high ranking officers from the police and a colonel and a lieutenant appeared, and there was a man in civilian clothes too; and while we were getting the key to open the gate for Father Mésidor, they broke down the gate and came in.

"What were they looking for? They were looking for Franck Romain's guy who had lost his armband, whom we were holding prisoner inside. So they released the guy and let him go. They claimed they were here to provide security, which wasn't true at all, because I saw them, they were the ones who ran the whole show.

"Chavannes Jean-Baptiste [head of the MPP] was also at the mass. He and Father Aristide and the other priests went upstairs [into the residence after the attack]. Mésidor came in with some others and went upstairs to talk with them. Eventually at around 1:30 p.m. the police evacuated the [100-150] people who were in the inner courtyard. They lined them up and sent them out into the street, and told them to walk, to get lost. The priests were still inside.

"After the police sent the people away, there were still some guys in civilian clothes with guns who stayed behind, the same guys who had attacked the church. They went upstairs and searched the rooms in the priest's residence, they searched and searched. They said they were looking for arms, a lie. They were a bunch of thieves, they took a lot of jewelry from the parishioners during the attack. "Give me your bag, give me your bag," they were saying, while they were stabbing people, killing them.

45

"So they searched, but they didn't find what they were looking for, they didn't find guns. They left instead with all the audio cassettes that Aristide had in his room. Eventually the Papal Nuncio came. Then the priests who were there, Mésidor, Nau, Aristide, Désir, they left in their cars, not with the police, who had already left. The priests locked up the rooms and the residence where they had been and they left with Chavannes Jean-Baptiste in their cars to go somewhere safe. The Papal Nuncio took them to a safe house."

Another eyewitness to the massacre at the church, a photo-journalist whom we know to be reliable, confirmed most of the details of this account.

E. The Avril Government

Despite vows by Gen. Avril to respect human rights and to reinstate the rule of law, and Gen. Avril's ratification of several international human rights conventions,* abuses at the hands of the army have not ceased. Although the brazen violence of the last week of Gen. Namphy's rule has not been repeated, killings and other violent abuses at the hands of soldiers and paramilitary forces continue to be a regular part of the Haitian landscape under Gen. Avril.

The targets of the violence under Gen. Avril are not significantly different from those victimized by the predecessor military governments. Peasant associations, labor unions, church groups and political demonstrations are most frequently selected. Occasionally, an outspoken critic of the government becomes the subject of violent attack. Common citizens also bear their share of violence -- because they cross a local section chief or military official, because they find themselves in the center of a land dispute, or because they happen to be walking down the streets of Port-au-Prince at the moment that unidentified gunmen take aim.

---

*   In early December 1988, the Avril government announced the ratification of the International Covenant on Civil and Political Rights; the International Covenant on Economic, Social and Cultural Rights; the UN Convention Against Torture and Other Cruel, Inhuman and Degrading Treatment; the Inter-American Convention to Prevent and Punish Torture; and the San Salvador Additional Protocol to the American Convention on Human Rights.

The responsibility for the violence has not always been clear under Gen. Avril. As the Avril government has established itself, however, the violence appears increasingly to be directed, at least in significant part, by the highest echelons of the military government.

During the initial month or two of the Avril government, a case could be made that regressive factions opposed to Gen. Avril were behind the political violence in an effort to destabilize the government and install a more right-wing head of state. This view was reinforced by the nature of the September 17 coup, led by junior officers who appeared to want to put an end to the shocking violence epitomized by the St. Jean Bosco massacre.

Since then, however, indicators of the origin of the violence point increasingly toward the National Palace. For one, in several well-publicized cases outlined below, victims were arrested by soldiers and brought to detention centers. Indeed, in one case, those arrested were brought to the National Palace itself and beaten there. The army's willingness to use official channels in attacking political opponents bespeaks confidence of high-level backing.

Even political violence of more ambiguous authorship increasingly appears to have government approval, as the Avril government persists in its refusal to prosecute or discipline offenders. Indeed, in only the rarest instances have troop commanders even acknowledged wrongdoing by their troops. The lack of prosecutorial redress amounts to a tacit sanctioning of this violence by the Avril government.

The growing contempt for the rule of law has also undoubtedly contributed to the ongoing "insecurity" in and around Port-au-Prince. Although the perpetrators of these killings generally are not known, the army's willingness to resort to and tolerate violence for political purposes can only embolden those behind the killings, regardless of their military connection.

In short, the honeymoon is over for the Avril government. The good will it garnered upon assuming power from the murderous Namphy government has long since been dissipated in a pattern of violence that increasingly bears the imprints of the same military that has ruled Haiti for the past three years. The head of government is certainly more clever than his predecessors, the facade he presents generally appears more benign, but the continuing political violence under his command evidences an unalloyed disdain for fundamental human rights and for the basic foundations of democratic government that is no different from earlier military governments. The following examples illustrate this pattern of abuses.

1. Attacks Against Outspoken Political Opponents

The most visible targets of political violence under the Avril governments have been outspoken critics of the government and its policies. These individuals have tended to be tied to mass-based movements such as labor and peasant organizations, or to reform factions of the army, and to lack the relative protection of a high political profile.

In a country where approximately 7,000 soldiers maintain control over six million people, the military perceives the prospect of mass mobilization of the country's poor, along with splits in its own ranks, as the greatest threats to its power. Most of the leading politicians who today are freely voicing critical opinions of the military do not represent such a threat. Separated from the Haitian masses by language, education, wealth and social background, they tend to lack the popular base that might threaten military dominance, and thus are left relatively free to express their opinions.

Those associated with popular movements, however, have found their ability to voice critical opinions seriously circumscribed. Because these cases test the true limits of the Avril government's tolerance of dissent, we view them as important indicators of the government's democratic intentions, in many ways a more significant indicator than the level of discourse at meetings of leading politicians in Port-au-Prince.

a. The Murder of Two Members of Vérité

During the night of November 26-27, 1988, a group of four plainclothesmen and a uniformed soldier killed Michelet Dubreus and Jean Félix. They also arrested Rock Mondésir without a warrant. The three men, residents of Cité Soleil on the outskirts of Port-au-Prince and members of a community organization known as *Vérité,* or Truth, had written a public letter to Haitian radio stations two days earlier identifying some of those believed to have participated in the St. Jean Bosco massacre and expressing concern at their presence in Cité Soleil. Witnesses identified the plainclothesmen as former attachés, a reference to armed, plainclothes forces that, at least through September 1988, had been affiliated with the Casernes Dessalines and *Recherches Criminelles*. Mondésir was held in a series of detention centers, including the Anti-Gang Investigations Unit *(Service d'Investigations Anti-Gangs)* (the new official name for *Recherches Criminelles)* and the supposedly closed Fort Dimanche, before being brought to the National Penitentiary, where he was kept until his provisional release at the end of January 1989.

b. The Arrest and Beating of Five Members of ANOP

On January 16, 1989, soldiers arrested two members of the National Assembly of Popular Organizations *(Assemblée Nationale des Organisations Populaires)* (ANOP), Vesnel Jean-François and Roland Pierre, who were writing anti-government slogans on walls and distributing anti-government pamphlets in Cité Soleil. The two were taken to the National Palace, beaten, and forced to spend the night on their knees holding rocks on their heads. According to Pierre, at the time of the arrest "one of the officers broke a branch off a tree and beat me over the head with it, causing two deep wounds." The next day they were taken to the Anti-Gangs Investigations Unit, where they were interrogated and again beaten. "They wanted us to name the leaders of ANOP and insisted that we were being paid for writing slogans on the wall, and so wanted to know how much we were being paid," reported Pierre.

Three days later, on January 19, after securing an appointment with Lt. Larochelle of the Anti-Gangs Unit to discuss the fate of the two detainees, the ANOP leadership delegated five of its members to the meeting. While they waited to meet Lt. Larochelle, two others -- Sgt. Déju and an attaché, Fritzner Exumé -- reportedly provoked a fight which lead to the beating and arrest of three of the ANOP delegation, Yves Sanon, Roland Paul and Alain Zéphyr. The three were detained overnight in the Anti-Gangs Unit, effectively changing places with Jean-François and Pierre, who were released a short time later. The next day, January 20, the three remaining ANOP detainees were brought before Judge Julien Eustache, who ordered their release.

49

c. The Killing of Luc B. Innocent

Luc B. Innocent, a minor presidential candidate in the November 1987 election and leader of the Revolutionary Union Movement *(Mouvement d'-Union Révolutionnaire)* (MUR), was killed on October 8, 1988 by an army patrol in Fonds-Verrettes in southeastern Haiti, near the Dominican border. According to a government communiqué, he was killed during an attempted take-over of the local military barracks. He allegedly was planning to launch an armed invasion to oust the Avril government, although he had crossed the border with fewer than 10 followers. The government has offered no proof of this alleged plan. Innocent's body was buried on the spot, without legal formalities or prior notice to his relatives.

One MUR party member who survived the military attack and fled to the Dominican Republic contradicted the official version. He said that troops, suddenly and without warning, attacked a hut in which Innocent and his followers had been meeting, killing Innocent and wounding others.*

Innocent spent years in exile in Venezuela. He returned to Haiti in 1986, and launched his campaign for the presidency in 1987. In April 1988, he was forced to flee Haiti, requesting asylum in the Dominican Republic, when the Manigat regime accused him of plotting its overthrow. In connection with this accusation, a relative of Innocent, a notary named Camille Muzac, was arrested and spent six months in detention without formal charges. The government's evidence at the time consisted of several empty bottles found in the courtyard of Muzac's house, which the government claimed Innocent was planning to use as firebombs. Despite requests from several Haitian human rights organizations, the Avril government so far has declined to investigate the killing of Innocent.

---

*   Haiti Solidarité Internationale, Bulletin No. 25, September 26-October 11, 1988.

d. The Arrest of 15 Soldiers of the Presidential Guard

During the weekend of October 15-16, 1988, the army arrested fifteen soldiers of the Presidential Guard. It also fired or forced into retirement several junior officers. All of these soldiers had actively participated in the September 17 coup that brought Gen. Avril to power. Those arrested were:

Sgt. Patrick Frantz Beauchard
Sgt. Pierre-Louis Faudresse
Sgt. Germain Sonthonnax
Sgt. Philemon René
Cpl. Vilex Saintil
Cpl. Althidor Jean-Alixon
Cpl. Septembre Luckner
Cpl. Timothée Jean-Frank
Priv. Delile Fricot
Priv. Jean Mathieu
Priv. Joseph Clébert
Priv. Figaro Gétry
Priv. Cangar Robert
Priv. Joseph Job
Priv. Oupette Gasner

The junior officers included Maj. Pierre Cherubin and Lts. Richard Salomon, Pierre Michel Lubin and Joseph Medard. They reportedly were forced underground after army units attacked their homes with machine-gun fire. Their removal and the imprisonment of the lower-ranking soldiers signaled a dramatic step backward for the Avril government.

Following September 17, Gen. Avril found himself pressed from all sides by rank-and-file soldiers seeking removal of their commanding officers. According to reliable reports, Gen. Avril suggested to some of the junior officers and soldiers listed above that they form an advisory committee to present the demands of the army's rank-and-file. The committee ended up ratifying the ousters of commanding officers and pressing for further reforms within the army, including the removal of high-ranking officers known to be involved in the lucrative drug trade. Committee members were also determined to

51

eliminate the paramilitary forces which had continued to function with impunity.

Sgt. Patrick Beauchard distinguished himself by taking the lead in initiating raids on known paramilitary headquarters and the residences of their alleged leaders. It is widely believed that he forced Col. Jean-Claude Paul to leave his command of the powerful Dessalines Battalion after storming with tanks and heavy weaponry the headquarters -- a house in the Delmas section of Port-au-Prince -- of a group of attachés linked to Paul. Reports that attachés had been launching their attacks on civilians from that house had circulated for months, but previous governments had taken no action. While this particular raid ended with only five arrests, the pictures of hundreds of attachés were recovered. Beauchard reportedly brought the five attachés he had captured to the government-owned television station and forced them to reveal their affiliation with Paul on a live broadcast. The same night, after several hours of high-level negotiations, Paul agreed to retire.

Gen. Avril and other top associates evidently saw such bold assertiveness as a threat to their rule, and began a campaign to discredit Beauchard and his allies. The government reportedly spread damaging rumors within army ranks, and it appointed Beauchard to head the National Lottery while spreading further rumors about alleged favoritism and corruption.

Although no formal charges were ever filed, the government alleged that these soldiers and officers had plotted its overthrow. Among the alleged co-conspirators was Col. Samuel Jérémie, who is serving a 15-year prison sentence for fatally shooting demonstrators in Léoganes in January 1986. Col. Jérémie had been briefly freed in the wake of the September 17 coup. No evidence of this alleged plot was ever presented, nor were the fifteen imprisoned soldiers brought before a court or permitted to see counsel. They were released in December, after significant pressure from human rights and democratic forces in Haiti. They had been held at the National Penitentiary in Port-au-Prince and were not reported to have been mistreated while in custody.*

e. The Arrest of Rockefeller Guerre and Sylvain Jolibois

On February 6, 1989, Rockefeller Guerre, head of the Union of Patriotic Democrats *(Union des Democrats Patriotiques)* (UDP), was arrested at his home at 6:45 a.m. by three men from the Anti-Gang Investigations Unit, two in uniform and the third in plainclothes. According to Guerre's wife, Guerre drove his car to police headquarters accompanied by two of the detectives; the third drove in a separate car with license plates indicating that it was a rented vehicle. Guerre reportedly spent five hours in the offices of the Anti-Gang Unit without being interrogated before being transferred to the National Penitentiary. In a statement to Radio Soleil, Port-au-Prince Police Chief Col. Georges Valcin charged Guerre with having been part of an attempt to place a grenade beneath stands erected on the Champs de Mars in central Port-au-Prince during the carnival celebrations. According to Col. Valcin, the police apprehended an unnamed individual who had been given the task of detonating the grenade, which in turn, Valcin implied without stating, led to the arrest of Guerre.

The timing of the arrest suggested that political motives were behind it. Guerre had joined in a coalition with two of the four leading presidential candidates of the aborted November 1987 elections, Sylvio Claude of the PDCH and Louis Déjoie of PAIN, in opposition to participation by democratic groups in the February 9 forum to discuss the Avril government's proposal for an electoral commission. To underscore this opposition, the coalition had called for a general strike on February 8 and 9.

---

*   A similar though shorter detention occurred at the end of October 1988. Port-au-Prince police chief Col. Georges Valcin announced the arrest of seven soldiers from Fort Dimanche who had called for the removal of their commander. They were, according to Radio Nationale: Jean-Baptiste Valere, Ruben Jean-Charles, Andre Sauveur, Elois Deraline, Armand Christophe, Alexis Dorelus and Joseph Jean-Baptiste. The seven reportedly were released in early November and expelled from the army.

Another outspoken opponent of the Avril government, Dr. Sylvain Jolibois, was arrested the same day as Guerre. Both Guerre and Jolibois were released on February 16 when charges were dismissed for lack of evidence.

2. Attacks on Freedom of Assembly and Association

Consistent with the military's apparent fear of popular mobilization, the army has repeatedly acted to stop or disperse political rallies and demonstrations. Not all rallies or gatherings have been barred; several have occurred without incident in Port-au-Prince and elsewhere. But evidently because of the potential for such demonstrations to mobilize broad popular opposition to military rule, they have been targeted for attack far more regularly than single outspoken political leaders.

The frequency of the military's intervention to stop demonstrations indicates that freedom of assembly and association exist today in Haiti largely at military whim. As the following examples illustrate, the government has shown no commitment to these freedoms as basic rights of the Haitian people.

- On October 6, 1988, a popular demonstration took place in Desdunes in the Artibonite to protest the inclusion in the Avril government of several figures who had been associated with the policy of terror under prior governments. One demonstrator, Evarold Racine, died, and many were wounded when a sergeant identified as Dutroit Valcourt opened fire on the demonstrators. On October 13, this same officer arrested without a warrant Dufort Chérilus, an inhabitant of the Artibonite village of Estère, because he had denounced the presence of paramilitary forces in the area.

- On October 9, 1988, in the course of a demonstration in Petite Rivière de l'Artibonite, Dieunoula Joseph was arrested and brutally beaten by soldiers identified as Cpls. Napoléon and Kébreau.

- On October 17, 1988, upon orders reportedly issued by the department's military commander, army troops prohibited a popular demonstration in Estère.

- On October 24, 1988, in Port-au-Prince, the police used tear gas to break up a demonstration organized by the Joint Committee of Democratic Forces *(Comité de Liaison des Forces Démocratiques)*. The demonstrators were demanding that Gen. Avril step down, that the 15 soldiers arrested on October 15-16 be released, and that Father

54

Jean-Bertrand Aristide, who had been ordered out of the country by the Salésian order, be permitted to stay.

- On October 24, 1988, in Port-au-Prince, a peaceful demonstration organized to demonstrate support for Father Aristide and to demand that the Avril government step down was dispersed with night sticks and tear gas.

- On November 29, 1988 the Federation of Neighborhood Associations in Cap-Haïtien organized a peaceful march of approximately 3,000 to commemorate the victims of the massacre perpetrated on the day of the aborted elections one year earlier. The military broke up the march with tear gas. The home of Dr. Charles Manigat, a well-known democratic figure who had run for senator under the banner of the FNC, was also attacked with tear gas. Manigat and the head of the Federation, Max Montreuil, had been arrested earlier that month on charges that they had been inciting rioting and the looting of the residences of a former Namphy government official. After being forced to spend the night in jail, they were released when the charges were dismissed for lack of evidence. Since then they have both been continually harassed by military authorities.

- On December 5, 1988, in Les Cayes in southwestern Haiti, the police prohibited a gathering that was to have occurred the next day to commemorate the massacre of peasants in nearby Marchaterre on December 6, 1929. The police also arrested two organizers, Father Rénald Clérisme and agronomist Harry Abel. The next day, December 6, the army fired shots into the air as it encircled the church in Les Cayes where a mass was being performed to commemorate the Marchaterre massacre.

- On January 26, 1989, approximately 500 factory workers went to the offices of the Ministry of Social Affairs in Delmas, in metropolitan Port-au-Prince, to settle a dispute with their employer. The employees of the Ministry evidently panicked and called the Leopard battalion of the army, which deployed troops to the scene. The Leopards encircled the crowd and began randomly beating those gathered. According to Col. Himmler Rebu, the Leopards were told that the crowd was going to burn down the office.

- In a confidential memorandum to Gen. Avril dated January 13, 1989 -- leaked to Radio Soleil at the end of January and later authenticated by the government -- Antony Virginie Saint-Pierre, minister of information and coordination, called on the Haitian armed forces to be placed on a state of alert against alleged efforts to destabilize the government in the Central Plateau, particularly the area around Hinche, Savanette, Belladère, Mirebalais and Thomassique. According to the memorandum, those behind the supposed destabilization effort were the MPP, the FNC (by then defunct), PUCH, the Charlemagne Péralte Front *(Front Charlemagne Péralte)* and the *Ti Legliz*. The evidence presented to demonstrate this alleged effort was thin, however: a certain Idly Cameau purportedly had traveled to Savanette to contact other named individuals and to ensure communication between Savanette and Mirebalais; the MPP allegedly had received funds from unnamed Belgian associations; and the FNC supposedly had distributed money to peasant groups and voodoo priests to help them commemorate an important voodoo holiday. The memorandum appears to have been initialed by Gen. Avril with a note that it should be discussed at a meeting of the army's general staff at 11:00 a.m. on January 20, 1989. At least several of the recommendations contained in the memorandum reportedly were adopted, indicating that the basic thrust of the memorandum was accepted. Among the actions taken were the sending of envoys to the Central Plateau to collect intelligence, the establishment of roadblocks to monitor comings and goings in the region, and the deployment of troops to Hinche to reinforce existing forces and to "sensitize the department commander to the political reality that is developing under his eyes." In the face of outcries and protests, the Avril government reaffirmed the Saint-Pierre memorandum. Then Defense and Interior Minister Col. Carl Dorsainvil stated in a communiqué that the government's investigation revealed "the existence of certain problems that truly deserve that urgent solutions be considered by the government to benefit the populations in question." Neither the problems nor the proposed solutions were specified. Faced with increasing protests and press inquiries, the Avril government's most recent explanation has been that it was "trying to prevent another Jean-Rabel," a reference to the bloody massacre on July 23, 1987, in which thugs loyal to wealthy landowners killed at least 135 members of a local peasant organization.

- On February 15, 1989, in Port-au-Prince, troops attacked a peaceful demonstration organized by the National Organization for the Defense of Youth *(Organisation Nationale de la Defense de la Jeunesse)* (ONADEJ), midway on their planned march from Bel Aire to the Palace of Justice. The youths were demanding freedom for jailed opposition leaders Rockefeller Guerre and Dr. Sylvain Jolibois and protesting the threats contained in the above-mentioned memorandum from the Information Minister. The troops attacked with tear gas and beat a number of demonstrators. Reporters covering the event were also assaulted, as detailed in Chapter V.

3. Land Disputes

In an overpopulated country, where erosion caused by deforestation and primitive farming techniques regularly reduces the amount of arable land, it is no surprise that much of the dispute over political power reduces to a dispute over land. In rural areas, local military commanders and section chiefs who have long profited from financial arrangements reached with large landowners have assumed the role of defending landed interests against peasant challengers. In this sense, the army in rural Haiti plays much the same role as it did under the Duvalier dictatorship -- a law unto itself in the service of the economically powerful.

The March 1987 Constitution was to have altered this rural power relationship by replacing the section chiefs with administrative councils under popular control -- the Administrative Councils of the Communal Sections *(Conseils d'Administration des Sections Communales)*, commonly referred to as CASECs. The failure to hold fair CASEC elections has meant that this project is unfulfilled, and that the law in rural Haiti continues to reside in the hands of corrupt military officials who for years have seen service to their pocketbooks as a higher duty than service to their constituencies.

The following accounts illustrate this pattern of military involvement in land disputes and the often-violent abuses that result:

- On October 27, 1988, in the course of a land dispute between two groups of peasants in Estère in the Artibonite, one group, armed with sticks and spikes, enlisted a Sgt. Charles and a Cpl. Rosemond. They then proceeded to kill three members of the opposing group -- Verité François, Luckner Noël and St. Jean Sylvestre -- and wounded five, including Dieuseul Jérôme, Jean-Baptiste François and Luckner François.

- On October 29, 1988, Jacques Philippe, a lawyer who was representing peasants from St. Marc in a land dispute with the town's section chief,

57

was killed by a man in uniform and a plainclothesman on his way from St. Marc to Port-au-Prince. The two assailants, who had ridden with Philippe since St. Marc, shot him to death in Bon Repos, 20 kilometers north of Port-au-Prince.

- On November 1, 1988, Jean Lacoste Edouard, a section chief in Petite Rivière de l'Artibonite, and his assistants, Fritz Alvarez and Méreste Fadaël, fired numerous shots into the air to force Lafrance Toussaint and Prédinord Louis to abandon a piece of property.

- On December 6, 1988, in Médor, in the sixth communal section of Petite Rivière de l'Artibonite, section chief Presendieu Merthus beat Grécius Francine in the course of a land dispute between Francine and two of Merthus's assistants, Clercius Piersil and Anilius Piersil. Francine took flight following the beating. On December 8, 1988, in Doddard, in the fifth communal section of Petite Rivière de l'Artibonite, section chief Nicolas Riche illegally arrested Vanes Sénadieu in the course of a land conflict with Terrilus Tuly, a large landowner in the region.

- On December 18, 1988, at the request of Jean-Norbert Montero, an ex-offical of the Namphy government, the section chief in Savanette arrested Lenord Petit Fabre, Desanord Joseph, Colobri Altenor, Montelis Petit Fabre and Dieurifils Saimphar. These peasants were arrested because they rejected and protested Montero's attempts to expel them from their land. Four of the five were released on December 26 following considerable public protest.

- On December 26, 1988, in Bois l'Estère, in the third communal section of Marchand-Dessalines, an assistant to the section chief known as Dieuliphète illegally arrested a man known as Chesnel following a land dispute between Chesnel and Dieudonne Jules, a large landowner in the region.

4. Military Thefts

Corruption and violence are linked not only in the context of land disputes. Increasingly, common thefts are reportedly committed by men in uniform. Their participation in this ordinary criminal activity is facilitated by the impunity seemingly accorded most soldiers before the law.

- On October 10, 1988, in Delmas, a uniformed soldier shot and killed Pasteur Rodrigue Renaud and wounded his companion, Lionel Saget. The soldier made off with over US$3,000.

- On November 22, 1988, in Port-au-Prince, 24-year-old Lesly Béjin was killed at approximately 9:00 p.m. by a group of uniformed men armed with Uzi machine-guns. The men had just committed a robbery and, after insisting that Béjin give them a ride in his car, murdered him.

- During the night of December 17-18, 1988, in La Vallée-de-Jacmel in southern Haiti, four individuals in green-olive uniforms, armed with revolvers, spikes and sticks, stabbed and beat Franck Léon, manager of the small cooperative savings fund in the town.

- During the night of December 21-22, 1988, in Port-au-Prince, a pawn shop named "Confiance en Dieu" was ransacked by a group of about a dozen, some dressed in green-olive.

- On December 23, 1988, on the rue des Miracles in downtown Port-au-Prince, Maret Louis was kidnapped as he left a bank by two uniformed soldiers. The soldiers drove Louis near the international airport, stole $640, and left.

5. Other Military Violence

It is a reflection of the breakdown in law and order as applied to military troops that often it is impossible to determine the motive for acts of violence committed by soldiers. Whatever the reasons behind the killings, shootings and beatings outlined below, these disturbingly regular incidents reflect indifference, if not encouragement, from the military high command. On several occasions, army troops have engaged in acts of violence for no apparent political or financial motive. The brazenness of these abuses reflects a disturbing willingness by the army to disregard the law, a willingness that continues under the Avril government.

- On October 21, 1988, an attaché of the Anti-Gang Investigations Unit wounded Alex Bernard with a gunshot.

- On October 23 1988, in the Bizoton section of Port-au-Prince, two armed men, one in a green-olive uniform, entered a house near the Nirvana market, arrested two men and two women, and drove toward the center of town. One man was killed, and his body dumped on the Bicen-

59

tennaire in downtown Port-au-Prince. The other man, Dorvilien Méry, was wounded. The two women were released unharmed.

- On October 24, 1988, Cpl. Delva Osius of the Fort Dimanche battalion murdered a young man known as By at Croix-des-Bossales on the outskirts of Port-au-Prince. The next day, Cpl. Osius beat a witness to the murder, Fritz Altidor.

- Also on October 24, in Cité Soleil, a sergeant from the Casernes Dessalines wounded Daniel Laurent with three bullets in the right hand and left side.

- At 5 a.m. on October 26, 1988, a uniformed soldier accompanied by two others wounded a man known as Jean-Claude with a gunshot to the back.

- On November 2, 1988, Roland Joseph, known as Roland d'Haïti, a former soldier widely believed to be a drug smuggler and assassin-for-hire, was shot to death with his maid by soldiers who were attempting to enter and search his house in Bon Repos, just north of Port-au-Prince. An official military communiqué reported that Joseph had been killed while resisting the soldiers. A mason working in the house, however, said that the soldiers found Joseph hiding behind a refrigerator and shot him.

- On November 23, 1988, in the Carrefour-Feuilles section of Port-au-Prince, a sergeant in the Presidential Guard known as Camy killed Edwine Petit Frère, an employee of the Ministry of Commerce and Industry, and wounded two others.

- On December 9, 1988, on rue Tiremasse in Port-au-Prince, Sgt. Macly Longchamps of the aviation corps fatally shot himself after a dispute with his mistress, Léonne Germain. The next day, December 10, soldiers from the aviation corps invaded rue Tiremasse, sealed off the neighborhood, and arrested and beat numerous residents and passersby, among them Gérard Paul, Pierre Joseph, Paul Ilrick, Frantz Paul, and Frantz Milord. In a highly unusual move -- apparently related to the fact that the soldiers' attack took place on the day that Gen. Avril announced the ratification of several international human rights instruments -- Lt. Col. Renan Jean-Louis, the commander of the aviation corps, later issued a press release stating that the soldiers had acted without his authorization and would be subjected to disciplinary measures. The soldiers were fired.

60

- On December 15, 1988, Clédanor Nonsant, having been arrested in November in Léogane and then transferred to Petit Goave (both in southern Haiti), died after brutal beatings in both towns by law enforcement authorities.

6. Unattributed "Insecurity"

As under other recent governments, "insecurity" -- the killing of seemingly random individuals by unidentified gunmen -- has become a recurrent problem under Gen. Avril. By definition, responsibility in these cases is difficult to determine. The correlation between the frequency of such killings and political tensions over the past year, in a country that traditionally had little common crime, suggests that political motives often lie behind the murders, even if the particular victims appear not to be chosen for political reasons.

One or both of two different groups are probably behind the killings. Just as forces loyal to Gen. Namphy appeared to have been behind the killings in the spring of 1988, so military or paramilitary opponents of Gen. Avril may be behind the killings today. Under this view, the killings are designed to destabilize the Avril government with the aim of replacing it with a more right-wing regime.

It may also, however, be in the interest of Gen. Avril and his allies that the killings continue. From their perspective, the killings have the advantage of terrorizing the population and thus discouraging organized opposition. Moreover, as Port-au-Prince police chief Col. Georges Valcin has done, the killings can be used to argue that existing police and military forces lack the strength to maintain order and thus that international aid must be resumed. (This argument conveniently glosses over the demonstrated ability of the army and the police to make a powerful show of force when they seek to prevent popular protests, as they did on November 29, 1988, the first anniversary of the aborted elections.)

Regardless of motives, however, the fact remains that the Avril government has encouraged the "insecurity" by its passive attitude toward violence generally. This is highlighted by its refusal to prosecute even the most egregious military and paramilitary violence. The following killings, reported by LAPPH and CHADEL,*nsecurity" under Gen. Avril's reign:

61

- On October 5, 1988, in a ravine in Delmas, a young woman was found bludgeoned to death.

- On October 12, 1988, three bodies were discovered in three different locations in Port-au-Prince: the rue du Quai, the rue Bonnefois and Croix-des-Bossales.

- On October 30, 1988, Jean Saintilus, a driver for CATH, narrowly escaped death when the car he was driving in Port-au-Prince was riddled with bullets fired by two unidentified men.

- On October 27, 1988, Thomas Nicolas, father of the army chief of staff under the Namphy government, Carl Michel Nicolas, was shot to death in his home.

- On November 3, 1988, on the Bicentenaire near the Ministry of Foreign Affairs in Port-au-Prince, the body of an unidentified young man was found dead of gunshot wounds. His hands had been tied.

- On November 14, 1988, in Léogane, the body of Marcel Jeanty was found having been stabbed to death.

- On November 16, 1988, at 10:45 p.m. in Carrefour, a group of armed individuals killed Philippe Overty and shot his wife in the left thigh.

- On November 24, 1988, two unidentified men were founded shot to death in front of St. Jean Bosco church in Port-au-Prince. Those who live nearby reported not having heard gunfire, suggesting that the two had been killed elsewhere and transported to the sight of the September 11 massacre.

- On December 2, 1988, a young man was found shot to death in Port-au-Prince on the road to the international airport.

7. Military Interference with Legal Process

Contributing to the ready use of violence in Haiti is a contempt shown by soldiers for legal processes generally. Both a cause and a reflection of the breakdown in the rule of law, this flouting of legal procedures continued under the Avril government. For example:

- During the popular reprisals against alleged participants in the St. Jean Bosco massacre following the Avril coup, soldiers handed over presumed participants to mobs for them to be killed and burned. In at least one instance, the soldiers finished off the presumed participant before delivering his body to the vengeful mob.

- On October 4, 1988, in Gonaïves, armed soldiers in uniform forced *Commissaire du Gouvernement* (the local prosecutor) Me. Dieuseul Placide to sign an order releasing from prison Auguste Magène, a former Tonton Macoute accused of murdering Makenson Michel, a schoolboy killed in November 1985 in the course of anti-Duvalier protests.

- According to CHADEL, at 2 a.m. on November 10, 1988, at 7 rue Oge in Pétion-Ville, four individuals were caught in the process of setting fire to a house. One was captured by neighbors and taken to the local police station. The police refused to take custody of the alleged arsonist or to charge him. With legal redress denied them, the neighbors took matters into their own hands and killed the man. The police then arrested five of the neighbors.

- CHADEL also reported that on November 28, 1988, on the Ile de la Tortue in northern Haiti, a soldier named Jean-Yves Théogène and two other soldiers arrested Henry Joseph, the justice of the peace of the town, after Joseph had rendered a judgment against the three soldiers. The soldiers took the justice of the peace before the local military commander.

- On December 10, 1988, soldiers of the region refused to bring Nateste Sintisma, an assistant of the section chief, before a tribunal to which he was summoned by the local *Commissaire du Gouvernement* Eddy Dupiton.

- On January 21, 1989, Mireille Delinois -- former wife of Col. Jean-Claude Paul, who died under circumstances suggesting poisoning on November 6, 1988 -- returned to Paul's home in Duplan, near Fermathe, accompanied by an attorney and a justice of the peace and armed with a court order permitting her to enter the house, which had been officially sealed, to remove her belongings. As the truck brought by Delinois was almost loaded, troops from the Casernes Dessalines arrived, apparently summoned by Claude's relatives, and prevented her from proceeding, in defiance of the court order.

IV. MISTREATMENT OF PRISONERS

During our August 1988 visit to Haiti, we requested permission to see four detention facilities in Port-au-Prince: the National Penitentiary *(Péniten-cier National)*, Fort Dimanche, Casernes Dessalines and the Criminal Investigations Unit of the Port-au-Prince Police Department *(Service des Recherches Criminelles)*. Our principal concern was to investigate reports that prisoners were being killed on a regular basis by torture and starvation in *Recherches Criminelles*. We also hoped to determine whether prisoners were severely mistreated in the other three facilities.

Our visit to the detention facilities was extremely abbreviated; we were given one day to visit three of the four facilities. Nonetheless, we were able to determine that torture and extreme mistreatment continued in *Recherches Criminelles* at the time of our visit. We were unable to draw definitive conclusions regarding the other facilities, for the reasons outlined below.

A. Recherches Criminelles

Recherches Criminelles, which, as noted, was renamed the Anti-Gang Investigations Unit *(Service d'Investigations Anti-Gangs)* following the September 1988 coup, is located in a yellow, low-lying building opposite the National Palace in downtown Port-au-Prince. The building houses offices and a small detention area. At the time of our visit, *Recherches Criminelles* was under the authority of Col. Joseph Baguidy. Following the September coup, Col. Baguidy was relieved of his duties and replaced by Capt. Coulanges Justafort. In November, Justafort reportedly was replaced by Maj. Eugene Jose.

Recherches Criminelles has long been notorious for the torture and killing that occurred there. In March 1986, reports began to emerge of gross mistreatment of detainees. More recently, CHADEL reported that the following prisoners had been murdered in *Recherches Criminelles* between April and early July 1988:

Victim	Cause of Death
Sanon Jean-Marie	Torture
Yvon Myrthil	Starvation
Malachie Bernardo	Starvation
Guito Louis	Starvation
Toussaint Amazan	Torture
Elie Joseph	Torture
Dieufils Germain	Torture
Elie Jeanty	Torture
Gabriel Chéry	Torture
Hubert Michel	Torture
Murat Jean	Torture
Kenol Clervil	Starvation
Gérard Cayo	Starvation
Jonas Lovinsky	Starvation
Onel Paul	Starvation
Ronald Bernard	Torture
Pierre (Last Name Unknown)	Torture
Camille (Last Name Unknown)	Torture

Similarly, in an October 1987 incident described in Chapter VI of this report, presidential candidate Yves Volel was murdered in front of *Recherches Criminelles* as he was about to enter the facility to investigate reports of abuse of a client being held there. A former *Recherches Criminelles* detainee, Yves Auguste, who was held there in March and April 1987, said he saw four brothers beaten to death for refusing to tell the police chief where they had hidden money they had been accused of stealing. And on May 17, 1988 Amnesty International reported that Rene Pierre Louis, an engineer, had been held for between five and six months at *Recherches Criminelles* without access to a lawyer. He was beaten on the buttocks, back, head, ankles and soles of his feet. Although the resulting wounds became infected, he was not allowed to see a doctor. Other such reports have emerged periodically.

66

With this history in mind, we pressed for an opportunity to investigate conditions within *Recherches Criminelles*. Brig. Gen. Fritz Antoine, then the Minister of Justice, gave our delegation written permission to tour the four detention facilities in Port-au-Prince which we had requested to see, including *Recherches Criminelles*. He also arranged for a civilian attorney from the Ministry of Justice to accompany us and to facilitate our entry into the facilities. Despite this attorney's presentation of a written authorization for us to enter *Recherches Criminelles,* signed personally by the Minister of Justice, we were denied entrance to the facility. Numerous plainclothes employees, known as attachés, lingered at the entrance while we were there. We suspect that the relatively impromptu nature of our visit accounted for the reluctance of the authorities at *Recherches Criminelles* to grant us admission; two weeks later, a delegation from the Organization of American States' (OAS) Inter-American Commission on Human Rights was admitted to the facility after substantial forewarning, by which time the facility had been largely emptied of inmates.

We were, however, able to obtain first-hand information on conditions in *Recherches Criminelles* by interviewing prisoners in the National Penitentiary who had been transferred from *Recherches Criminelles* just the day before our August 13 visit. Although the circumstances of these interviews were not ideal in that they took place in a large room filled with many inmates, we were able to interview the prisoners individually, with no guards present, and at a sufficient distance from other inmates to ensure a modicum of privacy. The information we were able to collect corroborated the horror stories we had heard about conditions in *Recherches Criminelles*. We repeat three accounts below:

- André Dalusma had just spent seven days in *Recherches Criminelles*. Interviewed while lying face down on a cot, he had buttocks that were so badly cut up and bruised from having been beaten with a baton that he was unable to pull up his pants. Dalusma reported that the beating, which occurred in the course of an interrogation, had been ordered by Capt. Justaford, and had been carried out by an unidentified attaché. Dalusma was given food and water during his stay at *Recherches Criminelles*.

- Wilson Desir, who had also just spent five days at *Recherches Criminelles,* had a visible bullet wound in his side. He reported having been shot

67

by a police officer while still in the street because his car had accidentally crashed into a police car. At *Recherches Criminelles,* in an initial beating, Desir had been hit, approximately fifty times by his estimate, with a baton on the side of his rib cage; four bruises were clearly visible on his side below his armpit. During a second beating, Desir reported being hit approximately twenty times with a baton on his buttocks. In a third beating, he said hands were clapped approximately ten times over both his ears. Desir was asked no questions in the course of these beatings.

- Yves Alexandre, who had just spent two days at *Recherches Criminelles,* reported having been hit three times in the head near his ear with the butt of a revolver. He had not been questioned and had been given nothing to eat.

We were also able to interview a number of other prisoners at the National Penitentiary who had been transferred from *Recherches Criminelles* some months before. These interviews were conducted in more suitable settings, without guards or other inmates presents. Among the reports we received were the following:

- Cador Deresil spent three months in *Recherches Criminelles* between February and April 1987, in a cell with thirty to forty others. While he was there, inmates died of torture or starvation on a daily basis. There was no water in his cell, and the guards gave him no food. Other prisoners in the cell who "had privileges" received food and water and shared it with their fellow inmates. Deresil's hands were handcuffed behind his back the entire time. He estimates he was beaten on average every other day, often by a group of policemen. The police often questioned him about politics. One time, the police tried to remove his fingernails with a pincer, but did not succeed. Another time, a policeman bit his right ear; the ear still bears a visible scar. Electric shocks were also applied, through a band attached to his head.

- Another prisoner, who refused to give us his name out of fear of reprisal, spent two months in *Recherches Criminelles* in February and March 1988. He was kept in an area that he estimated was meant to house 30 to 40 but in fact housed 140 to 150. Twelve inmates died during his stay, some during beatings and some during the night for lack of water. There was no water in the cell, and the authorities provided no food. The prisoner's wife came on a daily basis to provide food and water. The prisoner was beaten by a baton and was subjected to electric shocks, which were applied through rings attached to his fingers. The prisoner paid $1,000 simply to be transferred from *Recherches Criminelles* to the National Penitentiary.

- Jean Louis Sinell spent three months in *Recherches Criminelles*, during which he saw 24 people die. His hands were cuffed and irons were kept on his feet. He was beaten daily, and showed us scars on his neck, forehead, wrists and ankles. There was "practically no food" at the facility.

Col. Weber Jodesty, at the time the warden of the National Penitentiary, was extremely open and helpful in allowing us to interview prisoners of our choice. Upon request, he brought us to see the prisoners who had just arrived from *Recherches Criminelles*. According to a government official in a position to know, Col. Jodesty's cooperation may have stemmed from his desire to clean up *Recherches Criminelles*. This official informed us that Col. Jodesty had on several occasions refused to accept the transfer of prisoners from *Recherches Criminelles* who were almost dead and were being passed on to the National Penitentiary in the apparent hope that their deaths would not be attributed to *Recherches Criminelles*. In addition, at the time of our visit, Col. Jodesty was sending two members of his staff to attend classes on human rights at CHADEL. Unfortunately, shortly after the September coup, Gen. Avril removed Col. Jodesty from his post, transferring him to a desk assignment.

As noted, shortly after Avril's assumption of the presidency, *Recherches Criminelles* was renamed the Anti-Gang Investigations Unit and Capt. Justafort, who had ordered the beating of André Dalusma described above, was named the new commander. The Avril government vowed that the facility would no longer be used as a detention center. Nonetheless, there is evidence suggesting that the facility is still used and that the abuses of the past continue under the Avril government:

- On November 15, 1988, Phaël Joseph was arrested for a theft that had occurred in the store where he worked. Joseph was taken to the Anti-Gang Investigations Unit and held without any of the required legal documents being completed. Nine days later, on November 24, his parents recovered his body from the morgue of the State University Hospital in Port-au-Prince. The body reportedly bore signs of torture.

69

- On January 19, 1989, as noted previously, Ives Sanon, Reynald Paul and Alain Zephir, all members of ANOP, were detained and beaten at the Anti-Gang Investigations Unit. They had come with a judicial order to seek the release of two other ANOP members, Jean François and Roland Pierre, who had been arrested three days earlier for writing anti-government slogans on walls and distributing anti-government pamphlets. Francois and Pierre were beaten in the National Palace. The ANOP members reported that approximately 40 people were detained in the Anti-Gang Investigations Unit while they were there.

B. Casernes Dessalines

We were admitted to the Casernes Dessalines by the commander of the facility, Col. Jean-Claude Paul, who greeted us and spoke with us at length before personally giving us a tour of the facility.* A large, fortress-like facility located behind the National Palace, the Casernes Dessalines houses four infantry battalions, the 16th, 18th, 21st and 28th, which together account for approximately 800 troops. It also contains a small area for detaining prisoners.

The detention area is divided into two wings. One wing consists of two rows of ten cells each on either side of a long corridor which receives natural light. The second wing is subdivided into two areas, each containing the same number of cells as the first wing; only one of these areas, however, receives natural light. The cells themselves are no bigger than three feet by six feet and are secured by heavy metal doors painted black, which darken the interiors of the cells so that even in the areas where natural light shines, prisoners would have extremely limited lighting available to them.

No prisoners were in the facility during our tour. Col. Paul reported to us that the facility was no longer in use, and has not been used other than to detain a prisoner briefly while he is identified before sending him to regularized custody at the National Penitentiary.

Three pieces of evidence made us doubt Col. Paul's claim that the detention area was not then being used. First, as we drove into the central court-

---

* Col. Paul was later replaced by Lt. Col. Guy François. As noted above, Paul died, apparently by poisoning, on November 6, 1988.

yard of the Casernes, immediately in front of Col. Paul's office and opposite the detention area, we saw four or five uniformed soldiers with guns quickly ushering another four or five men in civilian clothes out of the detention area and into a waiting truck, which then drove out of the courtyard area. Although the men in civilian clothing were not handcuffed, their behavior was consistent with prisoners being quickly removed from their cells. Second, unlike the other portions of the detention facility, the set of cells which received no natural light emitted a tremendous stench, suggestive of recent occupation of more than a transitory nature, and the floors were wet with water, as if they had just been washed during the course of our interview with Col. Paul. Third, as Col. Paul brought us on a tour of the facility, he initially showed us only the portion of the facility which received natural sunlight. Not until an explicit request to see the rest of the detention area from members of our delegation who previously had visited all parts of the facility in March 1986 -- at the time when Gerard Gourgue was Justice Minister and a member of the CNG -- did Col. Paul lead us to the second wing.

The sole prisoner we interviewed at the National Penitentiary who had spent time incarcerated in the Casernes Dessalines was Joseph Douze. Douze said he spent approximately one month in April 1988 in a dark, six-foot-by-six-foot cell. He reported that four other people were kept in his row of cells, and that one was beaten daily. Douze, a dual US and Haitian citizen who was incarcerated on gun charges, was not beaten.

On September 2, 1988, in what turned out to be its waning days, the Namphy government made the unprecedented announcement that Lt. Antoine Metellus of the Casernes Dessalines was going to be prosecuted for having caused the death by torture of Schubert Jean-Baptiste, a 30-year-old employee of the government television station, who was arrested at his home by an armed civilian on August 20, 1988, reportedly because he owed Metellus money. An investigation was said to have begun. Neither the Namphy nor the Avril government has reported any progress in the investigation, and the whereabouts of Lt. Metellus are unknown.

71

C. Fort Dimanche

Fort Dimanche lies on the outskirts of Port-au-Prince, near La Saline and the factory of the Haitian-American Sugar Company (HASCO). Like other prisons, it is also home to an army battalion. Under Francois Duvalier especially, it was infamous as the prison where political prisoners were sent and in many cases never emerged alive. Its commander took his orders directly from the President-for-Life, although prisoners were also sent there by the chiefs of the Secret Police, the VSN, and the Presidential Guard. According to a former soldier who was stationed at Fort Dimanche from 1968 to 1984:

> "Virtually every morning Lt. Louis Joseph and Lt. Fred Delva interrogated prisoners. Beatings were a regular part of these interrogations, and torture frequently was too.... All of the prisoners, political as well as regular, were subjected to the 'interrogations'.... Prisoners were executed at Fort Dimanche between about midnight and one a.m., never during the daytime.... The holes into which the bodies fell as they were shot were a permanent fixture, already dug by prisoners. A few prisoners would then throw dirt over the bodies. The officers had flashlights which assisted during the executions. They did not check carefully to see if the people were dead, counting on the dirt to finish them off."

We did not receive a complete tour of Fort Dimanche. The military complex consists of an administration building near the entrance to the facility and two other detention facilities behind the administration building. Of the two detention facilities, we were only permitted to tour one, the newer facility on the left as one enters the complex. It consisted of approximately a dozen large cells which were empty at the time of our visit. Judging from the animal droppings scattered about most of the rooms of this facility, it had not been used for some time.

A delegation from the OAS Inter-American Commission on Human Rights, which toured Fort Dimanche in August 1988, was able to visit the entire facility. It reported encountering two prisoners in the second, older building.

The last time that Fort Dimanche was openly used as a detention facility was in June 1988, when at least 16 members and alleged associates of the government of deposed president Manigat, including members of his party, Rally of National Progressive Democrats *(Rassemblement des Démocrates Nationaux Progressistes)* (RDNP), were kept there for about one week. In an interview with New York-based weekly *Haïti Observateur,* Lionel Deschamps, secretary to the Manigat cabinet, reported that the detainees were generally not mistreated except that, during their first night in custody, they were forced to lie on the ground as soldiers stepped on them. On October 13, 1988, the Avril government announced that it would close this symbol of political killing and torture before January 1989, but as of the publication of this report, Fort Dimanche remains open.

D. The National Penitentiary

Because our time in the National Penitentiary was brief, we focused our attention on locating prisoners who could describe the atrocities taking place in *Recherches Criminelles,* which we regarded as our first priority. As a result, we were able to gather only a superficial, nonsystematic impression of conditions in the National Penitentiary. The largest prison structure in Haiti, occupying two city blocks in the middle of downtown Port-au-Prince, the National Penitentiary housed on the day of our visit 284 prisoners, according to Col. Jodesty, including 169 civilian men, 27 civilian women and 19 soldiers awaiting trial; and 62 civilian men, 3 civilian women and 4 soldiers serving sentences after convictions. Built during colonial times and partially restored during the US occupation of Haiti earlier in this century, the conditions were primitive. Of the approximately four women and eleven men whom we interviewed under conditions of privacy, away from any guards, none complained about mistreatment while housed in the National Penitentiary. We note, however, that we did not have time to conduct a systematic study of this issue, and others have reported beatings within the National Penitentiary. For example, according to CHADEL, Adolphe Mondelis and Jean-Claude Duperval were severely beaten on March 18, 1988 for having advanced unspecified complaints on behalf of fellow prisoners.

Another matter of concern to us, which we did not have time to investigate in the course of our brief visit to the National Penitentiary, is the practice

73

of confining prisoners for lengthy periods without legal process, in violation of both Articles 24 and 26 of the 1987 Constitution and Articles 5, 7 and 8 of the American Convention on Human Rights, which Haiti ratified in 1977.* In a May 6, 1988 report, for example, CHADEL listed 72 inmates at the National Penitentiary who had been held for up to 25 months without any legal order having been issued. Similarly, when the OAS Inter-American Commission on Human Rights toured the National Penitentiary two weeks after our visit, they were told by Col. Jodesty that there were 298 inmates in the National Penitentiary. However, a list given to them of inmates who were at some stage of legal proceedings contained only 165 names. The difference of 133 names appears to reflect inmates who are being incarcerated without any legal formality. Clearly, this apparent practice of detaining people for lengthy periods without legal process merits further investigation.

---

*   Article 24 of the Haitian Constitution provides in pertinent part: "Except where the perpetrator of a crime is caught in the act, no one may be arrested or detained other than by written order of a legally competent official." Article 26 provides in pertinent part: "No one may be kept under arrest more than forty-eight (48) hours unless he has appeared before a judge asked to rule on the legality of the arrest and the judge has confirmed the arrest by a well-founded decision."

V. ATTACKS ON THE PRESS

While the Haitian press operates without any formal or legal censorship, self-censorship is routinely practiced on issues of political sensitivity. Editors and station managers have experienced intermittent attacks on their reporters and premises since February 1986, and these have made them cautious of inflaming the army or the Duvalierist holdovers.

The military-dominated regimes that have ruled Haiti since February 1986 have alternated between tolerating a degree of outspokenness in the press and looking the other way as armed gunmen physically assailed the offending media. Buffeted by political currents out of their control and vulnerable to such armed attacks, Haiti's independent newspapers and radio stations have been forced to adapt, curbing their coverage of a variety of issues.

Haiti's domestic newspapers do little in the way of investigative reporting, rarely initiate stories and seldom interview ordinary Haitians. Coverage of stories outside Port-au-Prince is sporadic. In the place of hard-hitting reporting, the newspapers are filled with communiqués from the government and private organizations, columns of commentary, as well as sports, literary features and the like. The most incisive reporting, in *Le Nouvelliste,* for example, usually comes from the French news agency, Agence France-Presse (AFP). Newspapers are relatively expensive (60 cents an issue, as compared to an official minimum wage of $3 per day) and circulate almost exclusively in the capital.

The Haitian newspapers published in New York and Miami are freer to criticize the government and to report on topics considered too sensitive by the regular Haitian press. Their distribution in Haiti for the most part has remained free of interference.

With 80 percent of the country illiterate, the impact of the written press is limited to the educated elite. Haiti's radio stations are the most important medium for informing the populace, and they generally have been more courageous in their reporting than the printed media. The largest independent radio stations are Radio Soleil, the station of the Catholic Church; Radio Lumière, the station of the Protestant Church; and Radio Haïti-Inter and Radio Métropole, both unaffiliated. The reporters from these four stations are usually the only members of the national press to venture outside Port-au-Prince. Other independent radio stations broadcasting in Port-au-Prince include Radio Cacique, Radio Antilles, Radio Caraïbes and Radio Arc-en-Ciel. The government-run station is Radio Nationale.

In implicit recognition of the powerful role played by radio in Haiti, the independent radio stations have been the subject of several violent attacks at sensitive political moments, particularly during the week before the aborted elections of November 29, 1987 -- when assaults on the Haitian and foreign press reached an all-time high -- and in the week following the massacre of September 11, 1988 at St. Jean Bosco church.

In the period leading to the scheduled national elections in November 1987, the radio stations came under sustained attack, apparently because of their fairly extensive reporting on the campaigns of various candidates as well as their accounts of the violence directed against the CEP and other participants in the electoral process. These attacks included:

- On November 21, 1987, four armed men blew up the transmitter of Radio Lumière.

- On the eve of the scheduled elections, a squad of 16 uniformed army troops lobbed grenades and firebombs at the transmitter of Radio Soleil. The attack partially destroyed the transmitter and injured a watchman guarding the facility. The watchman later died of his wounds.

- Shots were also fired during the night of November 28-29 at the studios of Radio Lumière, Radio Antilles, Radio Cacique and Radio Haïti-Inter, forcing them to shut down, in some cases for several weeks.

By the time the polls opened on election day, November 29, only Radio Nationale and Radio Métropole were functioning in the capital.

In addition, both Haitian and foreign reporters who set out to witness the voting came under attack:

76

- At the polling place located in the Ecole Argentine de Bellegarde in Port-au-Prince, where some 14 voters were murdered, reporters arriving at the scene a short time later were fired upon by army troops in a gray jeep, according to Jean-Bernard Diederich, a freelance photographer for *Time* magazine. Dominican cameraman and reporter Carlos Grullon was shot at close range and died later that day. A British photographer, Goeffrey Smith, was wounded by gunfire. Two members of an ABC News camera crew, Javier Carillo, a Mexican, and Alfredo Mejia, a Salvadoran, and their Haitian driver, Franklin Ver, were also shot by a gunman who followed them to where they tried to hide behind a wall, "took careful and deliberate aim," and fired at close range, according to ABC correspondent Peter Collins. Other journalists jumped walls and hid in private homes to escape the shooting.

- Voice of America correspondent Greg Flakus and three other journalists were chased out of another Port-au-Prince voting station by pistol-firing thugs. They took refuge in a private home while the gunmen unsuccessfully scoured the neighborhood in search of them.

- Thugs knocked out Bernard Ethéart, a reporter for the Miami-based weekly *Haïti en Marche*, with a strong blow to the head.

- In one particularly chilling incident, Steve Wilson, an American freelance photographer, was accosted by four gunmen as he drove past a body lying in a pool of blood in downtown Port-au-Prince. Armed with two automatic rifles and two automatic pistols, the gunmen took Wilson's camera equipment as they forced him out of his car and on to his knees. One gunman bolted his rifle and was about to shoot when the group decided to heed Wilson's pleas for his life and send him back to his car. As he drove away, they blasted his windshield with gunshots.

After a day of such incidents, one veteran reporter remarked: "Press badges had become targets rather than shields."

Violence returned on January 17, 1988, the day of the substitute, military-run elections. Troops forced their way into the offices of Radio Arc-en-Ciel, a small station in Port-au-Prince, and destroyed its equipment. They accused reporters there of broadcasting a statement, allegedly from the banned independent CEP, annulling the day's vote. While such a statement had been sent to the radio stations, none had broadcast it, including Radio Arc-en-Ciel, sensing a trap.

During the short-lived regime of Leslie Manigat, two toughly worded communiqués were issued to the Haitian press regarding their reporting of the US investigation and indictment of Col. Jean-Claude Paul on drug-trafficking charges. On February 23, 1988, Brig. Gen. Carl Michel Nicholas of the Army High Command warned the press not to repeat "unfounded rumors," and on March 7, 1988, Minister of Information and Coordination Roger Savain warned the press that the government would not tolerate "cynical insinuations," "false accusations and public insults." The apparent motive for these warnings was that President Manigat, as he maneuvered to stay in power, had turned for support to powerful army factions led by Col. Paul, and, hence, could not tolerate open discussion of the charges.

The press responded to the warnings by curbing its coverage of Col. Paul's alleged drug trafficking. Radio Soleil, for instance, used only wire-service stories on the subject. Radio Haïti-Inter also limited itself to reporting wire-service dispatches, except that it took the added precaution of never mentioning Col. Paul by name, until the army issued a communiqué naming Paul.

The radio stations have developed various strategies for addressing other sensitive subjects as well. As violence in rural areas became a growing problem under the Manigat and Namphy governments, journalists reported on the situation but took steps to avoid themselves becoming victims. Reflecting the belief that factual reports of events would be deemed acceptable by those in power while opinions about those events might not, they eschewed overt editorials but engaged in a certain degree of investigative reporting, with the factual nature of the reporting providing a perceived cover for the value judgments implicit in the choice of topic. Other radio stations also adopted this strategy, but those that lack Radio Soleil's backing by the Catholic Church tended to be less venturesome in their reporting.

Travel by journalists outside of Port-au-Prince also at times was restricted. In August 1988, for example, a foreign correspondent was barred from traveling through the Central Plateau by the local military commander, Gabriel Pinasse, who claimed that a passport was needed, although none was legally required.

Not long after the massacre at St. Jean Bosco on September 11, 1988, armed individuals attacked the offices of Radio Cacique and Radio Soleil. A witness described one of the gunmen who attacked Radio Soleil as shouting, in reference to the station personnel, "it's the same band as Father Aristide, the same people who are bothering us."

Radio Cacique was attacked again on September 13, and much of its equipment was stolen or destroyed. When the incident was reported to *Recherches Criminelles*, the police called it unimportant and declined to investigate.

The government of Prosper Avril initially followed a hands-off approach to the media. As one of his first acts, the new minister of information and coordination, Antony Virginie Saint-Pierre, paid a visit to Radio Cacique, where he reportedly discussed the attacks on the station and pledged government support for rebuilding the station's facilities. The owners declined the offer out of fear of compromising their independence.

The Avril government has not, however, deterred continuing harassment and intimidation of the press, as the following encounters demonstrate:

- On October 14, 1988, following a minor incident involving a hawker of the daily newspaper *Le Nouvelliste*, three soldiers from the Casernes Dessalines who were summoned to the scene beat the newspaper's guard with nightsticks, thoroughly searched its print shop and briefly detained the guard together with Max Chauvet, the publisher of the newspaper.

- On October 15, Edouard Gaetjens of Radio Cacique and Manson Williams of Radio Haïti-Inter went to the military barracks of Mirebalais to interview troops. Soldiers there accused the reporters of having broadcast a report alleging that soldiers had accepted a bribe of $1,000 from the town's mayor to protect him from being "uprooted" -- removed from office, perhaps violently -- by the local population. Gaetjens was severely beaten.

- On December 21, 1988, in Port-au-Prince, Huggens Voltaire, a journalist for the weekly *Libération,* was brutally beaten by soldiers and armed plainclothes men in front of the National Penitentiary, where he was covering the release of 12 of the 15 soldiers imprisoned for purportedly plotting a coup. Voltaire was arrested and taken before Col. Christophe Dardompre, commander of the penitentiary, who ordered his release.

- On February 7, 1989, the commander of the military garrison in Hinche, Col. Ulysse Alcena, demanded that the Hinche correspondent for Radio Lumière, Delil Lexil, turn over a copy of a letter signed by 30 people criticizing the Avril government. The letter, which had been read over the air, protested the government's plans to repress an alleged peasant uprising in the Central Plateau as revealed in a leaked memorandum from the Information Minister. (See Chapter III.) When Lexil refused, Alcena threatened to close down the radio station. A week later, on February 14, three men in civilian clothes handcuffed an employee of Radio Luminère in Port-au-Prince after following him for several hours. They freed him only after he convinced them he was not a journalist.

- On February 15, 1989, in the course of breaking up a peaceful demonstration in Port-au-Prince, troops badly beat Thony Belizair, a reporter for AFP, as well as correspondents for Radio Cacique and Radio Arc-en-Ciel. Other journalists had their cameras smashed and film confiscated.

VI. FAILURE TO REDRESS PAST ABUSES

When the Haitian people overthrew Jean-Claude Duvalier in February 1986, they looked to the regime that replaced him to investigate the crimes of three decades of Duvalier dictatorship and to bring the culprits to justice. But the CNG and the military-dominated regimes that succeeded it showed little interest in delving into the misdeeds of those years, let alone in bringing charges against people who remained close to power in Haiti.

Most of the major figures implicated in torture and murder under the Duvaliers -- including Rosalie Adolphe, chief of the Tontons Macoutes, and Col. Albert Pierre, chief of the Secret Police -- were allowed to leave the country. The CNG's Justice Ministers made token attempts to force a few leading Duvalierists to stand trial. But only two important figures from the Duvalier era were ever found guilty and forced to serve a sentence: former Secret Police Chief Luc Desyr, and the particularly ruthless army Col. Samuel Jeremie. Even in those cases, the CNG presented a narrow case which avoided the full breadth of the defendants' crimes, with the apparent aim of not implicating those who remained in office.

The military's reluctance to take action on past abuses mirrored its own growing contempt for the rule of law. During the period of CNG rule, the brief Manigat months and the return to direct military rule under Gen. Namphy, the military remained largely above the law. Abuses in the countryside were particularly likely to go unpunished, and even in Port-au-Prince the rule of law was honored only in the breach.

In the wake of particularly heinous crimes that have been committed with disturbing regularity -- such as the massacre of peasants in Jean Rabel in July 1987, the murder of presidential candidates Louis Eugene Athis and Yves Volel in August and October 1987, the election day killings of November 1987, the murder of human rights lawyer Lafontant Joseph in July 1988, the killing of four members of a youth organization in Labadie in August 1988, and the mas-

81

sacre at St. Jean Bosco church in September 1988 -- the various post-Duvalier governments usually have called for investigations. To date, however, not one person has been arrested or charged in connection with any of these inquiries, leading to the conclusion that investigations are announced more to diffuse popular outrage than to identify and apprehend perpetrators.

The Avril government continued this trend in two reports that it released on November 15, 1988 -- one on the investigation into the widespread killing and terror that took place throughout Haiti on election day, November 29, 1987, and the other on the murder of presidential candidate Louis Eugene Athis on August 2, 1987. Although the first was written by a team of five men headed by a civilian and the second by a local military commander, both reflected a similar contempt for the norms of judicial inquiry as well as for the reader's common sense. They made a mockery of claims to objectivity and independence, ignoring readily available evidence, blaming the victims of violence, exempting the military from all culpability, and failing to identify a single person to arrest. Both investigations apparently had been completed and the resulting reports written within a month of the events they cover, but for unexplained reasons formal issuance of the reports was delayed in each case for approximately a year, although the report on the election day violence was leaked to the press in April 1988.

Gen. Avril's decision to release the reports without comment appeared to indicate support for their findings, while at the same time allowing him to test the waters before formally endorsing their conclusions. Once condemnations of the findings were heard from the democratic opposition in Haiti, as well as from concerned members of the US Congress -- who hold the key to resumed aid to Haiti -- Gen. Avril made a strategic retreat. On the eve of the first anniversary of the aborted November 29, 1987 elections, the Avril government annulled the findings of the report on the electoral violence which it had released just two weeks earlier. It called for a new five-member commission of inquiry presided over by a representative of Haitian human rights groups. The proposed commission would also include one representative of the press, one representative of the Bar Association and two representatives of the military government. The human rights community has called for major changes in the proposal to ensure the security of the investigators and to protect the independence of their inquiry. The Association of Haitian Journalists has endorsed the position of the human rights organizations, and the bar, claiming possible conflict of interest, has refused to participate on the commission. It remains unclear whether the proposed commission will be constituted.

While the call for a new investigation is welcome, the process leading to it does not instill confidence in Gen. Avril as a leader committed to punishing past abusers. That is all the more so because Gen. Avril did not rescind the report on the Athis murder, which, as we show below, was an equally objectionable whitewash.

Other official investigations, as detailed below, have yet to yield results. In the case of the St. Jean Bosco massacre, for example, the Avril government has obstructed efforts to bring the perpetrators to justice. Nor do other reportedly ongoing investigations reflect a determination to get at the truth.

A. The Report on Violence Surrounding the Elections of November 29, 1987

On December 3, 1987, four days after national elections had been violently aborted, the CNG issued a decree naming a commission to investigate the widespread violence surrounding the elections. Headed by Assistant to the Chief Justice of the Supreme Court Luc D. Michel, the commission also included Yvan-Richard Maurrasse, a lawyer in private practice who supervises the detention of prisoners at the National Penitentiary on behalf of the justice ministry; Ulrick Noel, another lawyer; and two army officers, Cols. Fritz Gourdet and Louis Thony Fils. The commission submitted its report to the CNG on January 15, 1988.

The report began by examining the social and political situation prevailing in Haiti before the elections, betraying a disturbingly limited view of democracy. Describing what it considered dangerous anarchy, the report condemned the fact that "improvised leaders have suddenly sprung up," "anonymous persons have declared themselves leaders of democratic groups," "radio and television stations have offered their time to all individuals who proclaim themselves democrats," and "strikes and demonstrations of all sort have become common occurrences." The report also blamed the CEP for its "patent hostility with regard to the Duvalierists" -- an allusion to the CEP's disqualification of 12 of the 35 presidential candidates because of their Duvalierist pasts -- without mentioning that the March 1987 Constitution, which was then in force, required the CEP to ban corrupt and abusive Duvalierists from competing in elections for ten years.

The army, on the other hand, was described as "not participating in the struggle for the conquest of power because it has never had political ambitions." Rather, the report concluded, the army undertook simply "to manage the transition and deliver power to a constitutional government established following elections." As detailed in Chapter II above, this surreal picture of the army's role in the electoral violence is contradicted in nearly every report on the elections issued by independent observers and journalists.

The official commission's report sifted through what it called the numerous "theses" regarding the play of forces behind the violence. It admitted a fondness for the idea that the extreme left was responsible but concluded that, "despite the attractiveness of this thesis, it does not hold up under examination...." The notion that foreign powers were responsible -- "through agents of the CIA in the heart of the CEP" -- was entertained but largely dismissed.

The conclusion reached by most independent Haitian and foreign observers -- that the violence was the product of collaboration between military and paramilitary forces -- was rejected: "Despite a meticulous investigation, the data collected does not permit one to establish that joint Macoute and army forces were involved in November's misdeeds." Notably, the only evidence that the report cited to support the "thesis" of Macoute-army collusion was an accusation by an anonymous US State Department official and the fact that troops from the Dessalines Battalion were providing security on the streets on the night of the violence. Inexplicably, the report neglected to take account of the numerous, well publicized reports by eyewitnesses that the election day violence was in many instances the product of uniformed soldiers working in tandem with plainclothes, paramilitary forces.

Moreover, the report took the next step of attempting to provide an excuse for the army in the face of widespread criticisms for its failure to halt the electoral violence. The report noted that, "on the government's side, the least intervention by the forces of order is openly criticized to the point where the power in place has often hesitated to take energetic measures in order not to deviate from the democratic line it assigned itself at the time of its investiture." As if this were not enough, the report also suggested that even if, hypothetically, individual soldiers might be found responsible for the electoral violence, "it is ... inappropriate to accuse the army as a whole -- despite the persistence of the CEP-CNG conflict -- of the electoral violence for which only certain elements, which it has been difficult to identify, are allegedly responsible."

Another theory, according to the commission's report, was that Duvalierist-Macoutes forces were responsible for most of the violence. The report implied, however, that if these forces were responsible, they had good reason to be concerned about the way things were going. In one of the report's most shocking passages, the killing of innocent voters is described as a kind of self-defense by Duvalierist forces:

> "It is conceivable that Macoutes and Duvalierists, collectively given no alternative but to struggle against banishment, might have been the authors [of the violence]. Decapitated, hunted down, persecuted, and burned alive after February 7, 1986, and in the face of the imminence of a resurgence of such acts following the results of last November's elections, out of a desire to survive, the Macoutes were conceivably forced to defend themselves."

The only evidence that the report cited of "the imminence of a resurgence" of acts of violence against Macoutes and Duvalierists was its authors' perception that the winner of the November 29 presidential election would have been Gerard Gourgue, the candidate of the FNC and the founder of the Haitian League for Human Rights, who the report said was "perceived as an anti-Duvalierist and anti-Macoutes alternative."

The commission was unable to conclude decisively who the authors of the violence were:

> "In this imbroglio, it is extremely difficult to locate individual actors, taking into account the insufficiency and incompleteness of the elements and clues turned up in the different interrogations. Despite rumors and accusations against certain

85

people, it has not been possible for the Commission, in an affair so serious, to designate the true authors, given the fact that the statements collected did not provide sufficient elements for appraisal."

The report went on to note that the commission was impeded in its work because many witnesses, including the members of the CEP, declined to appear before it. The CEP members, it should be recalled, had gone into hiding by mid-day on November 29, in fear for their lives.

Moreover, hundreds of reporters and official observers had flown to Haiti to witness what were supposed to be the country's first free presidential elections. None was interviewed by the commission, which noted only that:

"Although the media identified the perpetrators by name, it was not possible -- even after viewing the film of the massacre recorded at the Ruelle Vaillant [the Argentine school] -- to spot them. In the opinion of experts in cinematography, the film is, they say, a series of scattered scenes of the monstrous acts that occurred on Ruelle Vaillant."

The report observed that "the people interviewed are unanimous in recognizing the impossibility of identifying their aggressors.... They say these are individuals from other areas who perpetrated the crimes and acts of banditry on them. These last, as a group, were strangers to the region and for the most part were masked in a way to disguise their identity." This flies in the face of testimony by numerous foreign observers and journalists.

These "conclusions" were followed by a series of recommendations, including that the number of military personnel stationed in Haiti's cities be increased, that periodic searches for illegally held arms be conducted, and that reparations be paid to the victims of the November 29 massacre and their families. Since the report did not list the names of the people killed or wounded -- nor even give casualty figures -- it is not surprising that no "reparations" have been paid. The report also gave no indication of whom the commission interviewed or which methods of investigation it employed.

A leading Haitian human rights group, the Institute for Democratic Education *(Institute Mobile d'Education Démocratique)* (IMED), commented, "For all those who lived through that period in Haiti, this report is a slap in the face of the truth and also dishonors its sponsors and its signatories." The Haitians who braved gunfire and machetes that day to do something most Americans take for granted -- cast a ballot -- deserve better.

Although we fervently hope that the new commission of inquiry will be established and that it will be more successful in identifying the perpetrators of the November 1987 electoral violence, our hopes are tempered by the substantial obstacles that it will face, many of which have been imposed by the Avril government. First, the decree issued by Gen. Avril and his cabinet imposed a one-month time limit on the commission which, in light of the magnitude of the task confronting it, seems arbitrarily and unreasonably short, despite the widespread desire for speedy results. Second, because two of the five members of the proposed commission are to be members of the current military government -- a government which, in popular perception at least, continues to have links with members of the military who share responsibility for the November violence -- witnesses are likely to continue to be reluctant to come forward with evidence they possess. Third, unless the Avril government orders the full cooperation of top-ranking army officers who might have been involved in the electoral violence or who might possess information about those responsible for the violence, a source of information which in the view of many is crucial to understanding the cause of the electoral collapse will remain untapped.

In addition, Haitian human rights organizations have raised a series of legal concerns with regard to the proposed commission. For instance, they note that the decree limits the persons to be called in for questioning to those "who have been denounced by witnesses" and that, as a consequence, hearsay tes-

87

timony from victims of abuses and other witnesses, as well as other forms of proof, may be inadmissible, thus placing a severe evidentiary restriction on the commission's investigative abilities. In addition, mindful of past commissions that did not receive government protection in the face of violent attacks, such as the CEP, the human rights organizations have requested that the Avril government give strong guarantees that the safety of the members of the proposed commission would be assured. The Avril government has yet to satisfy these concerns. Quite apart from the form and powers of the proposed investigative commission, other potential obstacles remain. According to the Namphy government, the files of the original investigation are no longer available. In a meeting with our delegation in August 1988, Brig. Gen. Fritz Antoine, then Minister of Justice, informed us that the dossier of the investigation into the November 29 violence had been misplaced and that he had been unable to find it. Gen. Antoine may have made this statement in anticipation of a request by us to see the dossier, but it raises the possibility that the CNG or the Manigat or Namphy government saw fit to destroy some of whatever evidence had been collected.

Finally, it is possible that some of the participants in the electoral violence may now be dead. As noted, on November 2, 1988, Roland Joseph, known as "Roland d'Haïti," a former soldier widely believed to be a drug smuggler and a hired assassin, was shot by a military patrol at his house in Bonepos. Although the army claimed to have shot Joseph after he had thrown a grenade, witnesses on the scene describe the killing as a premeditated murder. One possible motive for such a murder would be the elimination of a witness who could have provided embarrassing testimony regarding the army's involvement in the drug trade and the November 1987 killings. The government has not officially refuted that account.

Similarly, the death of Col. Jean-Claude Paul four days later, on November 6, 1988, eliminated a military commander who is widely perceived as having significant knowledge about the source of the November violence.* Col. Georges Valcin of the Port-au-Prince Police Department reported that Paul appears to have been poisoned to death. The death is all the more suspicious because, according to Gen. Antoine during his meeting with our delegation in August 1988, Col.Paul was not interviewed regarding the November 29 massacre.**

B. The Report on the Investigation into the Murder of Louis Eugene Athis and Two Companions on August 2, 1987

While the violence of November 29, 1987 was viewed on television screens around the world, the murder of presidential candidate Louis Eugene Athis is less well known. Athis was a moderate politician who spent many of the Duvalier years in exile in the Dominican Republic, where he founded his political party, the Democratic Movement for the Liberation of Haiti *(Mouvement Démocratique de Libération d'Haiti)* (MODELH), to which he gained adherents largely among Haitians laboring in the sugar-cane bateys. Returning to Haiti

---

* That Col. Paul had been less than candid about the extent of the army's involvement in the violence of 1987 became clear to us during an interview that our delegation had with him in his office in the Casernes Dessalines in August 1988. When questioned about the involvement of troops from the Dessalines Battalion in the murder of scores of peaceful demonstrators in Port-au-Prince during the summer of 1987, Col. Paul suggested that provocateurs among the demonstrators must have been responsible for the murders. He reasoned that because the army's weapons are capable of firing 1,000 rounds per minute, hundreds, not scores, of demonstrators would have been killed if the army had been responsible. When we noted that the weapons he had mentioned were capable of firing not only automatically, that is, multiple rounds at a time, but also semi-automatically, that is, a single shot at a time, so that the army could well have been responsible for the killings, Col. Paul launched into a monologue to the effect that his soldiers were "not criminals," that they were "trained to protect the people," and that their "mission is to protect people not kill them." He concluded by noting: "A soldier will not shoot the crowd even if you order him to do so, because the people and the army are one."

** By contrast, Gen. Antoine indicated that Claude Raymond, a notorious Macoute leader who others reported seeing at the sight of the massacre at the Ecole Argentine, had been interviewed but that Raymond had denied involvement in the massacre.

89

after the downfall of Jean-Claude Duvalier, he soon declared his candidacy for the presidency and began campaigning in different parts of the country.

Athis and two supporters, François Jean and Oscar Dongerville, were stoned and hacked to death by a mob in the seventh rural section of Léogane, known as Aux Parques, on August 2, 1987. Athis had come to the area to campaign on behalf of his party.

Witnesses from Léogane have charged David Philogene, the local army section chief, with organizing the mob. A former Justice Minister under the CNG, François Latortue, who is a member of MODELH, has also accused Philogene of responsibility for the deaths. In a letter to then CNG Justice Minister François St. Fleur, Latortue wrote that Philogene "assembled a number of peasants, announced to them that enemies would be arriving in the village of Opac [Aux Parques] at around 12:00 p.m. on August 2 and asked them to sharpen their machetes and to arm themselves with clubs and rocks in order to exterminate the visitors." As the crowd attacked Athis and his aides, Philogene "was an undismayed witness to all this.... He did not sway or do anything at all to calm the fury of the peasants."

The government's report on these murders, based on an investigation conducted by Capt. Duvernac Renois, the army commander for the separate district of Croix-de-Bouquets, offered a very different view of events. It placed most of the blame for the killings on one of Athis's companions, Oscar Dongerville, who, as noted, was killed himself in the attack. The report claimed that Dongerville, as a native of the Léogane area, knew that area residents were fiercely anti-communist; that he knew the residents believed Athis's party, as well as Dongerville, were communists; and that Dongerville had received "warnings from two peasants that anyone in [his] company ... might be killed." Nonetheless, the report contended, Dongerville went ahead and brought Athis to the area for a meeting. "Mr. Dongerville wanted to gain personal profit from the presence of Mr. Athis," the report charged.

The introductory section of the report, which was written by Gen. Carl Michel Nicolas, then chief of staff of the army, summed up the investigation's findings this way:

"From the analysis of the facts, and comments by the investigating officer, it is evident that: 1) the inhabitants of "Chalette" (Léogane) did not know the leader Louis Eugene Athis, who they had never seen, but had a grudge against Oscar Dongerville, whom they accused of being a communist; 2) Oscar Dongerville, who has been a member of Louis Eugene Athis's party since Athis was in Santo Domingo, deceived the good faith and trust of Louis Eugene Athis and his companions by taking them to "Chalatte" when he knew very well that the inhabitants wanted to kill him and were calling him a communist; 3) that it was incredibly naive of leader Louis Eugene Athis to agree to go to "Chalatte" without having prepared the residents for a visit and despite warnings from two peasants that anyone in the company of Oscar Dongerville might be killed; 4) there was no premeditation in the case of the death of Louis Eugene Athis but rather a spontaneous reaction on the part of the peasants who had exhibited, since the anti-communist campaign of the 1970s in Haiti led by the late Gen. Bréton Claude, a certain aversion to this ideology which has already caused the death of several peasants."

Section Chief David Philogene was interviewed by the investigator, who gave great weight to his testimony. According to this testimony, Dongerville informed Philogene of the planned meeting and reported general hostility toward Athis's party in the Aux Parques area. Philogene testified that he took it upon himself to investigate the matter and obtained confirmation of the community's views when he overheard "some inhabitants working on two mountain tops speaking to each other." These people on the two mountains, he told the army investigator, were talking about how "Oscar had sold the Aux Parques section to the communists."

The report listed the names of a number of local people believed to have been involved in the killings, but said that these suspects all had gone underground when they received word that Philogene was planning to arrest them. To date, no one has been prosecuted. The sole responsibility that the report attributed to Philogene was a criticism for not having "been able to better penetrate the intention of the men he governs so as to discover in advance that they were planning to assassinate the unhappy Oscar Dongerville."

Philogene was given protection by the army when, following the September 17 coup, popular demonstrations in Léogane called for his indictment. The army resisted these demands and violently broke up some of the demonstrations. Philogene was dismissed as section chief on November 4, 1988, and briefly placed in custody in Léogane and then in Petit Goave. He was then freed, however, and on December 10, 1988, when the public prosecutor of Petit Goave issued a summons for Philogene to appear in court, he reportedly had fled to the Dominican Republic.

C. Continuing Investigations

The Haitian government claims to have ordered investigations into several other well publicized killings. These include inquiries into the killing of presidential candidate Yves Volel on October 14, 1987, and the murder of leading human rights attorney Lafontant Joseph on July 10, 1988. During our delegation's August 1988 visit to Haiti, we discussed the progress made on these investigations with then Justice Minister Brig. Gen. Fritz Antoine and several aides, including then *Commissaire du Gouvernement* for Port-au-Prince Mireille Pluviose.

Gen. Antoine began with vows of aggressive prosecutorial efforts to address past abuses. In language of a sort that has been repeated often by Haitian military officials but not followed in practice, Gen. Antoine proclaimed:

"This government is, above all, a government of openness, and it will remain that way, as we have nothing to hide.... Lt. Gen. Namphy, chief of state and head of government, has ordered that any act of vandalism be followed immediately by an investigation which is undertaken swiftly, impartially and independently; that all findings be made public; and that those found responsible be tried before a competent tribunal and judged according to the law.... Today, more than ever, the Republic of Haiti is and intends to remain the champion of human rights in the new world."

The actual progress of specific cases, as well as Gen. Antoine's accounting of them, reveal his words to have been hollow.

1. The Murder of Yves Volel

Yves Volel, a lawyer and presidential candidate, was shot in the head at close range as he stood in front of Port-au-Prince police headquarters. He died almost instantly. The killing took place as Volel, surrounded by several foreign and Haitian reporters as well as curious spectators, was attempting to call attention to the illegal detention and alleged mistreatment of Jean Raymond Louis, an activist arbitrarily arrested by the police who some days before had attracted Volel's attention by calling out from a cell window in *Recherches Criminelles.*

Outraged that such abuses were still taking place despite Haiti's Constitution and the legal rights due a detainee, Volel had announced to the press his intention to pressure the authorities into releasing Louis or bringing him to trial. With a copy of the Constitution in one hand and his lawyer's robe in the other, Volel had just started speaking to reporters when, according to journalists from Télé Haïti, plainclothes detectives armed with revolvers bolted out of *Recherches Criminelles* and started beating him. Two officers then deliberately executed Volel with two shots to the head and one to the heart. The reporters from Télé Haïti who witnessed the shocking event were also beaten, their equipment damaged and their film of the incident confiscated. Volel's body remained on the ground for approximately 45 minutes, allowing representatives of Haitian human rights organizations to view it and to confirm the details of the murder.

The Haitian military claimed that Volel had died in a gunfight. To support this claim, it pointed out that Volel had in his possession the handgun he habitually carried for protection. Segments of a film showing a handgun beside Volel's body were broadcast repeatedly on the government-controlled national television for days afterwards. But independent witnesses to the event refuted the police claim by noting that Volel never drew, let alone fired, his weapon. The attack by the policemen was unexpected, quick and brutal.

Asked by our delegation about the status of the investigation, Justice Minister Antoine said it had been largely completed, the murderers had been identified, but they had fled Haiti. He refused to reveal their identity, however, for the stated reason that the "investigation was still being pursued." Moments later, however, he contradicted himself, asserting that while the judicial inquiry was proceeding, there was little evidence available and nothing to warrant a major effort by the judiciary. As for the film that had been confiscated from the television reporters, Gen. Antoine said that he had no knowledge where this might be. When we asked to see the dossier of the investigation, Gen. Antoine and his aides strongly objected, stating that agreeing to such a request would constitute a breach of judicial protection.

Since the coup that brought him to power, Gen. Avril has replaced both Justice Minister Antoine and prosecutor Pluviose. During an interview with Jean Dominique of Radio Haïti-Inter, Gen. Avril said that he had seen the dossier on the Volel murder, that it seems that "the Ministry requested the dossier from the Port-au-Prince police and the police responded in turn that the investigation had been completed, that the culprits had been apprehended and convicted and that the case was closed." Gen. Avril did not identify who purportedly has been convicted, nor has there ever been any other suggestion that such convictions occurred.

2. The Murder of Lafontant Joseph

As noted in Chapter III, Lafontant Joseph, one of Haiti's leading human rights advocates, was found dead, his body mutilated, in his jeep on the morning of July 11, 1988. Our August 1988 delegation to Haiti questioned then Justice Minister Antoine on the progress made to date in the government's investigation of the Joseph murder. Gen. Antoine told us that the investigation had been held up because Joseph's relatives had been unwilling to cooperate. He asserted that the family knew that Joseph's death was not political but allegedly involved personal matters, a supposed affair of the heart, and he suggested that the crime might have been committed by a jealous husband or suitor. Gen. Antoine indicated that the police had found a woman's shoe and underwear in the back seat of the car in which Joseph's body was found. (A witness to the on-the-scene investigation conducted by the police on the day of the assassination told us that the police had placed a woman's shoe on the roof of the vehicle so that it could be plainly seen, but that it was unclear where the shoe had come from. The witness added that the police on the spot seemed to have immediately dismissed political motives for the murder. They continually talked about Joseph's alleged extramarital affairs.) Gen. Antoione seemed to dismiss the case off-handedly. He also asserted that many crimes alleged by the international press to be political are nothing more than individual settlings of scores.

During our meeting with the justice minister, we were shown a report of Joseph's autopsy, although the minister declined to give us a copy. The report we saw failed to note that Joseph's ear was missing, that his tongue had been cut, that he had been shot with one bullet or that his body showed a deep gash running from the oesophagus to the liver.

Following our interview with Gen. Antoine, we met with Joseph's widow, Raymonde. Contrary to the assertions of the justice minister, Raymonde Joseph was eager to talk about the murder and freely discussed it with our delegation. She strongly objected to the government's claim that she had refused to cooperate with the authorities and asserted that when she was contacted by the police, they were interested in pursuing only an alleged extra-marital affair as the cause of the murder. According to Raymonde Joseph, she told investigators that the owner of the bar in which Lafontant Joseph had last been seen alive indicated that Lafontant Joseph had left the bar around midnight on July 10 with two men and a woman.

Events following Joseph's murder do not support the government's characterization of it as a crime of passion. As noted, anonymous threats against the church where mass before Joseph's burial was to be said caused the cancellation of the service. To date, no official report of the Joseph murder has been released, nor has a perpetrator been identified or apprehended.

3. The Attack on the Church of St. Jean Bosco

Gen. Avril entered office promising to investigate the bloody massacre at St. Jean Bosco church which had precipitated his rise to power, but his government has taken no meaningful steps in this regard. Immediately following the September 17, 1988 coup, crowds in Port-au-Prince summarily murdered, and then burned the bodies of several individuals believed to have participated in the massacre. At times those meting out this "popular justice" were aided by uniformed soldiers, who turned over alleged participants in the massacre to the avenging crowd, and in at least one case killed the supposed participant first. Despite our horror at the St. Jean Bosco massacre, we must also condemn these summary executions. Because there was no investigation or trial, there was no way of ensuring that those killed had actually participated in the massacre. Nor did the revenge killings contribute to establishing responsibility for the massacre. Summary justice of this sort can no more form the basis of a lawful society than can the brazen killing at St. Jean Bosco that gave rise to it.

Without excusing this murderous retaliation, however, we note that the military-dominated governments of the past three years bear much of the responsibility for the popular perception that such summary killings are necessary. With their legacy of fruitless -- or non-existent -- investigations into killings by military and paramilitary forces, it is not surprising that segments of the Haitian population felt the need to take "justice" into their own hands.

Despite its lofty pronouncements, the Avril government has done little to correct that popular perception. As noted in Chapter III, during the night of November 26-27, 1988, armed plainclothesmen led by a uniformed soldier murdered two members of a popular organization called *Verité* -- Michelet Dubreus and Jean Félix -- who had signed a public letter identifying participants in the St. Jean Bosco massacre. A third member of *Verité*, Rock Mondésir, was arrested and delivered into military custody. To date, the Avril government has not announced an investigation into these murders or the arrest of the participants, despite the fact that the government must know, at the very least, who delivered Mondésir to military officials. Gen. Avril's implicit condoning of this murderous reaction to those who dare to bear witness to the St. Jean Bosco massacre hardly inspires popular confidence in his intention to establish the rule of law.

With this background, it is also not surprising that Gen. Avril faced widespread criticism for his decision to grant a safe conduct out of the country during the night of December 31, 1988-January 1, 1989 to former Col. Franck Romain, the former mayor of Port-au-Prince and the alleged mastermind of the St. Jean Bosco massacre, who had taken refuge in the embassy of the Dominican Republic following the September 17 coup. The military government issued an explanation of its actions in a written statement dated January 6, 1989, published in the January 7-9, 1989 edition of the government newspaper *L'Union*. Signed by Serge Elie Charles, minister of foreign affairs and religion, and Antony Virginie Saint-Pierre, minister of information and coordination, the statement justified the granting of the safe conduct by reference to Article 12 of the Inter-American Convention on Diplomatic Asylum, which provides in pertinent part: "Once asylum has been granted, the State granting the asylum may request that the person under asylum be allowed to depart the foreign territory, and the territorial State is under obligation to grant immediately, except in cases of force majeure," the safe conduct.

In an effort to deflect charges that the Avril government should have made its own, independent judgment about the appropriateness of granting asylum to an alleged mass murder like Romain, the statement referred to Article 4 of the Convention, arguing:

> "Others have maintained that asylum should not have been granted, since crimes that are pretty much matters of ordinary criminal law are involved. In this regard, the text of Article 4 is precise. In fact, it stipulates: 'It is up to the nation that grants asylum to describe the nature of the crime or to pass judgment on the reasons for the pursual.'"

Because the Dominican government had granted Romain asylum and requested a safe conduct for him on September 17, 1988, the authors of the statement reasoned, the Haitian government had no choice but to agree to the request:

> "It is therefore in taking strict care to respect the international commitments of the Republic of Haiti that the Haitian Government decided to accede to the Dominican request. No responsible government could do or try to do otherwise."

This legal analysis fails to relieve the Avril government of responsibility for its decision to grant Romain the safe conduct. To begin with, the Dominican Republic has entered a reservation to the principle contained in the Convention that the State granting asylum has the right to make that decision unilaterally. The reservation states:

> "The provisions of this Convention shall not be applicable, ... insofar as the Dominican Republic is concerned, to any controversies that may arise between the territorial State and the

97

State granting asylum, that refer specifically to ... the nonexistence of a true act of persecution against asylee by the local authorities."

Accordingly, contrary to the Avril government's statement, there was no duty to grant the Dominican request for a safe conduct. If the Avril government had contested the Dominican grant of asylum, it would have been within its right, given the Dominican reservation to the Convention, to refuse to grant a safe conduct. The Avril government's decision to grant the safe conduct nonetheless was thus a political, not a legal, matter.

Moreover, the Avril government's legal analysis ignores the steps that it could have taken to encourage the Dominican government to withdraw its request for a safe conduct for Romain. A government truly intent on prosecuting Romain would have rapidly completed its investigation, issued arrest warrants, presumably for Romain and others, and exerted as much public pressure as possible on the Dominican government to permit prosecutions to go forward. Instead, the Avril government sat on its hands and then secreted Romain out of the country while most Haitians were ushering in the New Year. Not until a popular uproar followed this move did the Avril government announce that it was seeking Romain's extradition, a belated request which the Dominican government reportedly has rejected.

We also feel compelled to comment on a rumor circulating in Port-au-Prince that the Avril government granted Romain a safe conduct in return for a promise from the Dominican government, as yet unfulfilled, to permit Dr. Paul Etienne to return to the Dominican Republic. Etienne, acting coordinator of the Good Samaritan Center *(Centre Bon Samaritain),* a Haitian medical and human rights organization based in Santo Domingo that concerns itself with the plight of Haitian sugar-cane workers in the Dominican bateys, had been expelled from the Dominican Republic on December 9, 1988. That unjustified expulsion should have been firmly and publicly protested in its own right until it was corrected, a step which the Avril government has not taken. Although we are unable to ascertain the accuracy of the rumor about the deal for Romain, we note that it would be insulting to the victims of the St. Jean Bosco massacre to equate the righting of the wrongful Etienne expulsion with the freeing of their alleged murderer. If the rumor is true, the Avril government's willingness to sell Romain's freedom so cheaply underscores once more the shallowness of its commitment to justice and the rule of law.

VII. ECONOMIC BACKGROUND

Although many of the human rights violations of the past three years occurred against a backdrop of competition for political power, economic issues often stood just behind the political stage. Political power in Haiti has long been an avenue to personal wealth, and the past three years are no exception to this rule. But just as the pocketbook motivated much of the violence before and since Duvalier's departure, so the suspension of international aid, as well as other possible economic sanctions, hold the key to convincing the army to relinquish power to elected, civilian authorities. Because of the importance of these economic matters, we devote a chapter to tracing their role in recent events, particularly since the collapse of the November 1987 elections.

A. The CNG's Economic Policy

Since the fall of the Duvaliers, Haiti's traditional agricultural base has been substantially weakened. The policies of the CNG, in particular, nearly crippled an agricultural economy that already was plagued by soil erosion, deforestation and primitive methods of farming. The Duvaliers' tight controls on imports, while enriching a minority, had had the secondary effect of providing a small economic space for domestic farmers to eke out a living. The CNG lifted these controls, flooding Haiti with contraband products. While the military profited by organizing the smuggling, and the poor saw a temporary drop in the cost of certain basic products, Haiti's farmers found that they could not compete with "Miami rice" or even imported US and Dominican sugar.

Contraband had a similar effect on Haiti's tiny industries. Even manufacturers of such low-technology products as clothing have been forced to fold up shop because of increased competition from imports of used American clothing.

As for Haiti's much-vaunted assembly industry, which was to have been the engine for sustained growth, it has functioned to provide work at low wages

101

for some 40,000 people, but little else. There has been virtually no secondary investment in Haitian businesses that might service or provide components to the assembly industry.

The near collapse of Haiti's economy accentuated the elite's long-standing dependence on government-related sources of income: corruption, embezzlement, smuggling and the siphoning off of foreign aid money. The departure of Jean-Claude and Michèle Duvalier, the largest siphoners, opened up new sources of wealth to Haiti's new military rulers. The CNG's economic policies heightened the military's dependence on those sources, with a corresponding disincentive to renounce this new-found wealth to reform-minded civilians.

B. The Suspension of Aid

The collapse of the November elections brought, in reaction, an immediate and substantial drop in the level of foreign economic assistance to Haiti. This strategy was well conceived because it struck at the financial incentives behind the military's violent obstruction of democratic reform.

In the aftermath of Duvalier's February 1986 fall, the United States had doubled its economic assistance and begun a new military aid program. Other countries had followed its lead and modestly increased their assistance. Taken together, aid from the United States, the Federal Republic of Germany (West Germany), France, Canada and the European Economic Community (EEC) accounted for approximately $175 million in 1987, with the United States contributing 61% of that amount, or $107 million.*

This increased aid had helped offset the cut in revenues that occurred when the Haitian government divested itself of such public enterprises as the

---

*   According to a Canadian parliamentary group that visited Haiti in March 1988, West Germany provided $26 million in aid, Canada $15,695,000 and the EEC $7 million. Other donors included the United Nations Development Program, which planned to give $31 million for the period 1987-1991; the International Monetary Fund, which had extended $33 million to alleviate Haiti's balance-of-payment deficit; and the World Bank, which planned to devote $80 million to Haiti for major infrastructure projects. In addition, in 1986 the Organization of American States created a priority inter-american aid fund for Haiti of approximately $673,000.

Darbonne Sugar Refinery and ENAOL, the essential oils refinery; eliminated export taxes on coffee and other agricultural and industrial products; and removed most restrictions on imports.

The drastic cut in U.S. assistance following the violent crushing of the November 1987 election has had a marked impact on the Haitian economy. It has also led other donors to review their assistance.

According to Richard Holwill, Deputy Assistant Secretary of State for Inter-American Affairs, the aid suspension resulted in the "curtailment of almost $60 million in economic assistance for fiscal year 1988."[*] The US Agency for International Development (USAID) reported the suspension of $30 million in Economic Support Funds, which provided balance-of-payment support to the Haitian government; $14 million in development assistance; $18 million in food assistance under PL 480, Title III, which the Haitian government was permitted to resell to Haitians, making use, with certain restrictions, of the profits to meet its balance-of-payments deficit;[**] and $1.6 million in soybeans

---

[*]   Testimony before the Subcommittee on Western Hemisphere Affairs of the House Foreign Affairs Committee, March 23, 1988.

[**]   According to USAID, "Title III provides needed food commodities to Haiti in the form of grants as long as the counterpart funds generated by commodity sales are used for approved economic development purposes. This program serves to bind USAID and the GOH [government of Haiti] into a joint program for agricultural policy reform and economic development." A Food Aid Strategy for Haiti: Maximizing Developmental Effectiveness, A report of the Technical Support Mission to USAID/Haiti, p. 69. USAID estimated that the sale of $15 million worth of commodities generated $17 million in counterpart funds.

to compensate for reduced US sugar imports. In addition, $1.2 million in military aid was suspended.

Most of the remaining US contribution to Haiti, approximately $26 million, was devoted to development projects run by private voluntary organizations. These funds were not suspended. They included development assistance of approximately $18 million and food assistance of $7.8 million under PL 480, Title II.* The aid suspension also did not affect approximately $600,000 in assistance to the Haitian government in connection with a drug and migrant interdiction program.

By causing Haiti's balance-of-payments deficit to rise from $40 million to an estimated $100 million, the aid suspension had the collateral effect of halting a planned loan from the International Monetary Fund (IMF). The IMF had been scheduled to release $17 million of a "structural adjustment facility" (part of an economic austerity package) to Haiti on December 14, 1987. Tied to the IMF money was another $20 million in credit from the World Bank, which was also withheld.** The US Economic Support Funds, the World Bank and the

---

*   Title II provides food aid through private voluntary organizations in Haiti. Four agencies administer most of this aid in Haiti: Care, Catholic Relief Services, Adventist Development and Relief Agency, and the World Food Program of the United Nations. Title II food grants take the form of Food for Work (a much contested program in Haiti because of its detrimental effect on Haiti's domestic agricultural sector), maternal and child health projects, and school and pre-school feeding projects.

**   Peter Ford, "Haitians feel the aftershock of US aid cuts," The Christian Science Monitor, December 22, 1987. According to the World Bank, the planned $20 million loan would have been the second installment in a $40 million economic recovery loan agreement signed in Washington in January 1987. An initial $20 million installment under this agreement was given in April 1987. In addition, in 1987 the World Bank gave Haiti a $20 million loan for transportation projects and a technical-assistance loan of $3 million.

IMF loans together accounted for approximately 30% of the Haitian government's $240 million annual operating budget for 1987.*

Other donors did not suspend their assistance to Haiti, although they did blame the military for much of the November 1987 violence. Canada, for example, in a posture that was typical of other donors, maintained that its aid program was essentially humanitarian, and that a cut-off would unjustly punish impoverished Haitians. Those opposed to continued Canadian aid pointed out that the assistance was channeled through the Haitian government, which had various means at its disposal to siphon off funds.**

Under pressure from the Haitian community in Montreal and several Canadian development agencies, Canada agreed to review its assistance. A Canadian parliamentary delegation visited Haiti in March 1988 under the Manigat government and concluded that Canada should continue providing aid through its established agreement with the Haitian government. It reasoned:

> "The only institution capable of proposing a master develop-
> ment plan for a country is its own government, particularly if
> it is an elected government. Notwithstanding its technical fail-
> ings, its degree of corruption, the poverty and scarcity of its

---

*   Id. The multilateral development banks also delayed consideration of the following loans to Haiti: a $40 million road project under consideration at the Inter-American Development Bank and a $24 million power loan under consideration at the World Bank. In addition, the World Bank had scheduled for consideration sometime after 1988 a $15 million power loan and a $124 million industrial-recovery loan. The US contribution to the government standing alone accounted for approximately 12% of the government's operating budget. Clara Germani, "Putting the Squeeze on Haiti," The Christian Science Monitor, July 5, 1988.

**   Representatives of the CED in Canada alleged that much of the Canadian aid was siphoned off by government officials. They accused the government of mismanaging programs, regularly overestimating budgets, using fraudulent receipts, overcharging for the cost of materials and equipment, and illicitly using vehicles. "Memoire du CED du Canada à la Commission Parlementaire devant voyager pour Haiti," presented February 18, 1988.

human resources, the government is the official seat of authority. An immediate dialogue must therefore be established and maintained with the government, and any decision to support its methods and practices must be made as circumstances arise. The Government of Canada has always been critical of Haitian governments and of their lack of policy in such key areas as human rights and democratic process."*

The Canadian delegation also recommended that Canada "seriously consider the possibility of substantially increasing its assistance through a rural integrated regional development project, taking into account the absorption capacity of the designated region and the executing agencies."**

Caribbean countries tried to respond to Haiti's political crisis, but with mixed results. While the Caribbean countries themselves make a relatively small contribution to the Haitian economy, they wield significant influence on other governments with considerable economic ties to Haiti. Immediately after the crushed November elections, some Caribbean leaders, with the aim of isolating Haiti internationally, openly called for the imposition of economic sanctions in addition to the aid suspension, and for the withdrawal of Haiti's observer status in the Caribbean Economic Community (CARICOM). These efforts were undercut by then Prime Minister Edward Seaga of Jamaica, who visited Haiti on December 10, 1987 and, after discussions with Gen. Namphy, dismissed the electoral violence as "history" and endorsed the CNG's substitute electoral plan, which ultimately led to the fraudulent installation of the Manigat government. Later intensive lobbying by the United States contributed to a lack of consensus among Caribbean nations, so that efforts to impose sanctions and withdraw

---

*   Report of the Parliamentary Group on Haiti, submitted April 26, 1988, p. 25. Canada finally announced that it would suspend its assistance to Haiti after the military government expelled Father René Poirier, a Canadian missionary based in the town of Grand Goave, on August 5, 1988.

**   Report of the Parliamentary Group on Haiti, p. 31.

Haiti's observer status in CARICOM came to naught. Significantly, however, Trinidad and Tobago refused to extend diplomatic recognition to the Manigat government.

The Haitian government responded to the aid suspension by cutting its budget by $25 million: $13 million was eliminated from the recurrent budget and $5 million from the development budget; and a scheduled $7 million payment to service Haiti's debt was suspended.* Once Leslie Manigat assumed the presidency, then Foreign Minister Gerard Latortue was quickly sent on a fundraising mission to Europe, Asia and North America, which produced a $4 million low-interest loan from Taiwan. Venezuela, which had endorsed the Manigat government, agreed to assist Haiti by constructing 150 housing units for use by the military, providing approximately 7,000 barrels of oil a day, installing an oil refinery, and providing 700,000 gallons of asphalt for road construction.** And France agreed to extend an emergency grant of $1 million for road construction. But these contributions were not enough to offset the country's increasing economic and political difficulties.

The government also tried to reduce the projected deficit by increasing taxes on income and consumer goods, hoping to generate about $15 million in revenues. In addition, it reduced by approximately half its consumption of oil. Despite the budget shortfall, the Manigat government avoided laying off government employees, which would have been a politically risky measure given Manigat's lack of popular mandate. However, meeting monthly payroll expenditures became increasingly difficult.

The Manigat government also tried to increase revenues from customs duties by assuming control of the ports with the aim of curbing pervasive smuggling. These efforts ended when they met with substantial resistance from the local military authorities who controled these ports.

---

*   Analyse sommaire de la situation economique (October 1987-March 1988)," Bulletin de la Banque de la Republique d'Haïti, No. 15, July 1988, p. 55.; "Quand l'Economie Haïtienne touche à sa Fin," Haïti Information Libre, No. 35, p. 9.

**   "Quand l'Economie Haïtienne touche à sa Fin," Haïti Information Libre, No. 35, p. 10.

For example, in St. Marc, located on the west coast approximately 60 miles north of Port-au-Prince, a large demonstration was organized in protest against the government's anti-contraband measures. In one of the few demonstrations permitted under Manigat, local military authorities were seen leading the estimated 3,000 demonstrators, who openly called for Manigat's overthrow. Customs inspectors sent by the government to take control of trade were sent fleeing by local authorities.* No attempts were made to limit the influx of contraband in other ports where smuggling had become a way of life, including Miragoane, Petit-Goave, Jeremie, Jacmel, Cayes and Cap-Haïtien.

With foreign reserves dwindling, the Manigat government was faced with the prospect of being unable to import basic commodities. This, on the one hand, would have increased the risk of popular rebellion, and on the other, would have made the military begin to lose patience with the Manigat experiment. At this point, the Commodity Credit Corporation of the US Department of Agriculture stepped in and provided a $9 million loan guarantee to US exporters, which permitted the Haitian government to purchase $2.5 million of rice, $1.5 million of lumber, $3 million of wheat, and $2 million of other commodities. In addition to permitting the Haitian government to import needed commodities, the loan guarantee replenished the Haitian treasury by allowing the government to resell the commodities at a profit.

Following the coup of June 19-20, 1988, which sent President Manigat into exile and returned Gen. Namphy to the head of the government, France and Venezuela announced the indefinite suspension of their aid programs. The Venezuelan troops sent to Haiti to help build housing units were quickly recalled. West Germany suspended its $3.5 million of assistance indefinitely. Among the affected projects were the construction of two hydro-electric plants and the rehabilitation of the electrical facilities of the town of St. Marc.

---

*   Haiti Solidarité Internationale, No. 15, May 16-23, 1988.

C. The Deteriorating Haitian Economy

Despite the unprecedented foreign assistance delivered to Haiti in 1986 and 1987, the economy has stagnated. In its annual economic report published in February 1988, Haiti's central bank stated:

"Production in volume of coffee and cacao decreased respectively by 20.3% and 7.1%.... The peasant, far from regenerating the production of export crops, devotes himself essentially to the cultivation of subsistence crops."*

"Sugar production has passed from 41.3 thousand metric tons in 1985-1986 to 32.5 thousand in 1986-1987, a decease of 21.3%."**

"Soap and cooking oil production have decreased by 39.7% and 36.4% respectively."***

In addition, manufacture of cloth for the Haitian market plummeted by 75%, from 452.3 to 112.3 million yards. The industry, which was forced to close its doors temporarily in 1987, was unable to compete with the massive im-

---

*   Banque de La Republique d'Haiti, Rapport Annuel, February 1988, p. 25. For more than five years, World Bank and USAID experts recommended that the Haitian government eliminate the tax on coffee in order to encourage peasants to move from subsistence to export farming. Even after the Haitian government removed the export tax, however, and despite USAID expenditures of approximately $9 million in support of greater coffee production, these objectives were not met because the principal beneficiaries of the tax cut were exporters and middlemen rather than peasant producers.

** Id. at 30.

*** Id.

port of clothing, most of it second-hand, that is readily available throughout Haiti. Haiti's small, largely foreign-owned export industry also had a mixed record. While factories producing clothing, toys, sports articles, handbags, travel bags and rubber goods prospered, other manufacturing plants closed up shop and moved to countries offering greater political stability.*

One development which temporarily eased economic pressures on the urban poor was the increasingly unrestricted flow of contraband in the form of foreign consumer goods.** All of Haiti's ports, with the exception of Port-au-Prince, had been closed to foreign trade by the Duvalier government. Following the overthrow of the Duvalier dictatorship, the ports were reopened on a *de facto* basis, without formal government approval. This irregular status, and a lack of official presence at the ports, contributed to an explosion of contraband, often with the support of local military authorities. A new local economy based on contraband goods has emerged, stimulating new needs and creating new jobs. The central government, with its embryonic customs bureaucracy, has proved unable to staunch this flow.

---

*   Id. at 34. "The economy remained stagnant as a result of coffee export declines, contraband, the disappointing performance of assembly exports, and the cessation of foreign assistance disbursements caused by the disruptions in the second half of 1987. Real GDP [Gross Domestic Product] growth in FY [Fiscal Year] 87 was estimated to be only 0.5%." USAID/HAITI, FY 1989/1990 Action Plan, p. 4.

**   The term contraband generally refers to the illegal import of foreign goods without the consent of government authorities. In Haiti, however, contraband often enters the country with the consent of senior military and government figures, but in violation of Haitian law. The result is essentially an open market, regulated by supply and demand. Such smuggling is not a new phenomenon in Haiti. During the Duvalier era, it was practiced by a few high-level government officials and some well-connected members of the Haitian business community. In 1986, it took on new proportions and was, so to speak, "democratized." Contraband goods are sold openly on the streets of Port-au-Prince and other cities. These goods enter through ports that are well known and open for public inspection.

The smuggled goods include rice, sugar, beans, cooking oil, canned milk, canned juices, chocolate, tomato paste, beer and malt, dried soup, alcoholic beverages, meat, poultry, cigarettes, used clothing, plastic shoes, detergents, soap, toothpaste, chairs, mattresses, radios, fans, bicycles (often stolen), motorcycles, used cars, tires and auto parts. At times, heavy machinery, petroleum and chemical products also enter the country outside legally prescribed channels.

Smuggling is not only done through Haiti's provincial ports. Most of the sugar brought into the country comes from the neighboring Dominican Republic. And some heavy machinery comes untaxed directly through the Port-au-Prince port facilities, the only ones equipped to handle heavy container loads. It has been estimated that contraband accounted for approximately $100 million in trade in 1987.*

While the flow of contraband goods created new jobs for urban dwellers,** and drove down consumer prices, its effect on agriculture has been quite detrimental. The huge volume of cheap "Miami rice" coming through the port of Gonaïves, for example, quickly began to endanger the revenues of the rice producers of the Artibonite valley. Although rice mills were functioning below capacity, depots were full and a portion of rice stock was being sold at a loss or falling prey to rats.*** This situation provoked so-called rice wars between the urban poor of Gonaïves and the peasants in the Arbonite valley.

The unrestricted import of Miami rice caused more than a drop in revenues for rice producers. Haitians tended to substitute cheaper Miami rice

---

*   "[USAID] estimates 30% of the rice consumption (approximately $16 million for FY 1987), 28% of flour consumption ($9 million), 20% of sugar consumption ($17 million), $1.7 million in wheat, $1.2 million in cooking oil, which along with other products would account for 20% of all imports, "are contraband. Denise Douzant Rosenfeld, Notes sur la Contrebande: Haiti Zone Franche: les effets du commerce ouvert, Report on an August 1987 mission, p. 5.

**   USAID estimates that more than 100,000 intermediaries exist.

***   Id. at 6.

for maize and sorghum, thus reducing the production of those cereals. Contraband flour also affected production of flour at the state-owned flour mill, the Minoterie, which possesses an official monopoly on the import of wheat, and through which most US food aid to Haiti was delivered. Because the Minoterie was forced to compete on the open market -- bags of flour were being offered at $4 to $5 less than the Minoterie's wholesale price of $22 a bag -- it was forced to reduce its prices. In June 1987, the Minoterie's production of flour fell to 40% of its capacity.* With the cut in US food aid under Title III, it has fallen even further.

In mid-January 1989, the Avril government announced several measures to control the flow of foreign goods to Haiti. These measures immediately met with strong protests and several demonstrations have been held against their imposition.

D. Future Prospects

The Haitian economy is now in a perilous state. Inflation is rapidly rising. The value of the Haitian currency, the gourde, has plummeted relative to the dollar. Within a period of five days in November 1988, the discount rate for gourdes on the parallel market for dollars jumped from 23% to 30% of the face value.** There has also been a rise in the retail price of basic necessities. In the last few months of 1988, the price of corn meal jumped 50%, Miami rice 33%, and charcoal 50%. The price of a pound of sugar rose by 50%.***

The cash-starved Haitian government has been periodically forced to suspend payment of salaries to its employees. Particularly affected have been employees of the health and education ministries. Yet the Avril government has

---

*   Id. at 8.

**   The gourde is officially pegged to the dollar at a rate of five-to-one. However, a parallel market has developed through which the real value of the gourde can be measured. In late 1986 the discount rate hovered around 9%, meaning 5.45 gourdes would purchase one dollar. Today, the dollar is worth 6.5 gourdes.

***   Roosevelt Jean-Francois, "Au board de l'explosion sociale," Haïti en Marche, November 23-29, 1988.

presented a budget of $270 million for 1989, with a special emphasis on public works programs. Gen. Avril also recently convinced the Haitian business community to agree to provide $15 million toward construction of housing units for the military, although many observers doubt that the business community will carry through on its pledge.

Despite the legislated suspension of direct aid, the United States has appeared willing to accommodate itself to the Avril government. In October, the State Department, in consultation with Congress, authorized the US Department of Agriculture to provide a loan guarantee of $10 million to US exporters to Haiti. The loan guarantee enabled the Haitian government to import wheat and then resell it at a profit, generating needed cash. "We are encouraged by what the Avril government is doing," an American official said, "and we're trying to do what we can within the limits of the restrictions."*

Yet it is increasingly clear that, despite Gen. Avril's vows to put Haiti on an "irreversible path to democracy," and the very public meetings he has held with Haiti's democratic leaders and other sectors of Haitian society, there has been little in the way of concrete and specific steps taken to respond to the basic demands of the Haitian people. The analysis made by the members of the Committee for Democratic Unity *(Comité d'Entente Démocratique)* during the short-lived Manigat era thus still rings true today:

> "Haiti today faces immense difficulties. Because of an inadequate legal system for land rights, a low level of technology, and poor fiscal and pricing policies, the agricultural sector is unable to respond to the needs of the population.
>
> "The industrial sector and the service sector absorb neither the surplus labor in the agricultural sector nor the increase in population. Poverty rises daily, and with poverty, tensions within society increase. Our society, politically weak,

---

*   Joseph B. Treaster, "U.S. Mellowing Toward Haiti, Releases some aid," The New York Times, November 20, 1988. The Reagan administration also released approximately $15 million worth of gourdes which were the proceeds of the CNG's earlier sales of food donated by the administration under the PL 480 program. US law governing such proceeds gave the administration little choice but to release the money to be spent on a series of development programs and other projects agreed to by the Haitian and U.S. governments.

economically backward, and socially unjust, has up to now demonstrated that it is unable to resolve its basic problems other than through two means that are equally unacceptable and revolting: a) the fierce migrations of the braceros [Haitian sugar-can cutters in the Dominican Republic] and of the boat people; and b) the brutal and unrestrained violence of the type seen on November 29, 1987.

"Any foreign assistance that would not place as its highest priority a preliminary and profound discussion of these problems, or the release mechanisms of which were not conceived with enough flexibility to verify its evolution through time, would amount to purely and simply condoning the coup of November 29 [1987], and the mascarade of January 17 [1988]."*

Renewal of foreign aid to Haiti, whether by the United States or other donors, and the establishment of a sound economic policy that would radically reverse current downward trends, must depend on the establishment of democracy and human rights in Haiti. That Haiti, the poorest country in the Western Hemisphere, is in desperate need of foreign assistance is not a subject of dispute. But in the past, foreign aid donors have generally considered development projects in a vacuum, disregarding the political factors that created kleptocratic despots who bankrupted the economy, and thus reinforcing anti-democratic tendencies. The Duvaliers and a few cronies -- aided by Gen. Avril, Haiti's current president -- siphoned off millions of dollars of international assistance to their private foreign bank accounts while major donors tolerated the attendant corruption, human rights abuses and lack of democratic freedoms. Development assistance to Haiti will have little effect as long as foreign aid donors continue to conceive of their programs in the absence of the political reforms needed to ensure the success of those program.

As outlined above, the economic recovery program adopted in 1986 and 1987 by the Haitian government at the urging of the international aid agen-

---

*   "Aide Internationale et Developpement," Declaration of MIDH, PDCH, FNC et PAIN to the Canadian parliamentary delegation, March 15, 1988, republished in Le journal du Commerce, June 13-20, 1988.

cies has been a failure. Marc Bazin, former Finance Minister of Haiti and a past World Bank official who is currently the leader of MIDH, underscored the political reasons for this failure when he said:

> "In our opinion, the absence of an adequate institutional framework is undeniably one of the major causes of the repeated failures of this type of program. The weakness here stems from the belief that one can undertake any policy, including a policy to correct the imbalances, with any government, including the one that created the imbalances.... How does one hope to be successful in implementing a recovery program when the political will is severely lacking?
>
> "Unlimited belief in the effectiveness of proven formulas, or a simple assumption that the sheer power of the sponsoring organizations will always prevail in the final analysis? Without a doubt, there's a little of both. But, in our opinion, in either case, what is less satisfactory is the underlying idea that a country's development might proceed without its leaders or, worse, in spite of its leaders. This is evidently a mistake. The other idea behind such an approach is that 'these leaders, we can ask them anything, because in the final analysis, they only represent themselves.' This unfortunately is often true. How then does one guarantee that the foreign resources are not just a substitute for the outflow of funds that would take place some other way? And where is the popular will in all of this muddle?"*

Given Haiti's history of official plunder, and Gen. Avril's widely acknowledged involvement in it, it is difficult to imagine that the current government will distinguish itself from its predecessors. Moreover, in view of the absence of basic reforms in public administration, and the continued presence of Duvalier and Namphy government officials in key posts, the Avril government increasingly gives the impression that it is exploiting the current economic

---

*   Marc L. Bazin, President of MIDH, "Pour une politique a visage humain," September 1, 1988, pp. 8-9.

115

crisis to justify inaction in severing itself from its Duvalierist roots. These observations simply underscore the need for establishing democracy and the rule of law before development programs stand a chance of succeeding. We hope that this crucial political component of Haiti's economic crisis will be addressed by those who seek to lift Haiti from its crushing poverty.

VIII. US HUMAN RIGHTS POLICY IN HAITI

The Reagan administration's policy of trusting the Haitian military to usher in elections, established since the ouster of "President-for-Life" Jean-Claude Duvalier in February 1986, took a dramatic turn with the administration's commendable decision to suspend most direct aid to the Haitian government following the military and paramilitary assault on the elections of November 29, 1987. That decision, later reinforced by Congress with mandatory legislation, provided Haitian democrats with their principal leverage to encourage the military to respect human rights and initiate a democratic process.

Unfortunately, the Reagan administration at times appeared not to have learned the lesson of its misguided trust in the Haitian military. At key moments the administration showed itself willing to renew economic support for the government after only superficial changes. Moreover, the administration, and especially its ambassador to Haiti, wasted their considerable moral authority by failing consistently to speak out against abuses. This lack of resolve in pressing for democracy and human rights appears linked to a desire to maintain close ties with a military that is seen as more likely than possible civilian alternatives to maintain "stability," to resist perceived leftist tendencies, and to cooperate with Washington in stemming the flow of refugees and narcotics to US soil. The resulting policy of ambivalence and contradiction risks repeating the errors of the first two post-Duvalier years, when the Reagan administration's eagerness to believe military pledges of support for a transition to democracy led it to ignore conflicting behavior and to back a government that became increasingly repressive.

In suspending aid following the carnage of November 29, 1987, the State Department proclaimed that, at the very least, "the electoral process [would have to be] resumed and restored" before aid could be reinstated, and that "an independent Electoral Commission is a key to restoring the electoral

117

process." In addition, the State Department noted "other measures that are crucial to Haiti's transition to democracy, [including]: the arrest, prosecution and punishment of those responsible for the election violence, the maintenance of public order, and the protection of Haitians during the election period as well as respect for the results of the new elections."

With these clear conditions attached, the suspension of aid created a major economic incentive for the CNG to reverse tracks, reinstate the CEP, which the CNG had dissolved on election day, and hold new elections under CEP auspices. Following its original announcement of the conditions for restoring aid, however, the administration was far less firm in insisting on the restoration of a credible electoral process. When the leading candidates from the November 29 elections called for reinstatement of the original CEP, as the Constitution required, the administration refused to endorse the demand. To the contrary, the State Department urged the leading candidates from the aborted November contest to participate in the proposed substitute elections, scheduled for January 17, 1988, despite the military's domination of the new electoral council it had created and its issuance of a new electoral law which, among other things, eliminated the secret ballot.*

Congress took a less equivocal view of the military's effort to control the elections. In December 1987, it passed legislation reinforcing the suspension of most aid to the Haitian government until "the democratic process set forth in the Haitian Constitution approved by the Haitian people on March 29, 1987, *especially those provisions relating to the provisional Electoral Council,* is being fully and faithfully adhered to by the Government of Haiti" (emphasis added).

When the four leading presidential candidates, representing an estimated 80% of the anticipated November vote, resisted the Reagan administration's urgings and announced that they would boycott the January 17 elections, the State Department, to its credit, announced on January 14 that "the

---

* "Haiti Opposition Urged to Field Unity Candidate," The Los Angeles Times, December 27, 1987 (AP)(quoting Deputy Secretary of State for Inter-American Affairs Richard Holwill)

118

way [the elections] are set up [is] flawed" and that it was "hard to see how [those elections] could meet ... the requirements that have been set forth by the Congress and our law now for the resumption of aid." At the same time, however, the administration undercut this stance by informally communicating the view that it would be willing to work with the victor, provided that he was not too closely linked to the Duvalier dictatorship and that Haitians appeared to accept, even reluctantly, the outcome of the flawed election.* The latter "condition" was so malleable that it easily conveyed the message that a populace which had been cowed into silence by the CNG's reign of terror would be deemed to have accepted the election results.

On January 17, as noted, the overwhelming majority of Haitians boycotted the voting, and fraud was pervasive. In Port-au-Prince, the streets were virtually deserted; the main exceptions were paid, often underaged voters being trucked from polling place to polling place for multiple cracks at the ballot box.

The Reagan administration failed to follow its pronouncement that the elections were "flawed" with the logical next step of calling for new and fair elections. To the contrary, the State Department issued a carefully guarded statement the next day which laid the groundwork for its willingness to work with the army's choice of "victor." While noting that "the results [were] clouded by the lack of a secret ballot and the absence of those candidates who earlier had demonstrated significant appeal to the voters," the State Department went out of its way to remark that "some Haitians did vote." And in notable understatement, the State Department concluded that "it is not possible to portray Sunday's voting as *fully* free and open" and that "the quality of these elections does not allow us to put Haiti in the category of countries that have *completed* a transition to democracy" (emphasis added).

When, after a week's delay, Leslie Manigat, reportedly a Reagan administration favorite in the aborted November contest, was named the winner

---

*   See Don Bohning, "U.S. role is small as junta prepares new Haiti election," The Miami Herald, January 14, 1988; Dan Williams, "U.S. Ready to Live With Haiti Election Result," The Los Angeles Times, January 9, 1988.

119

of the January electoral charade, the administration resisted pressures building in Congress to impose additional economic sanctions as an incentive for new elections. Instead, the administration affirmed its willingness to work with the Manigat government. In a statement issued on January 25, 1988, the administration praised the new president as "a distinguished political scientist with a long record of opposition to dictatorship," while referring to the compromising circumstances under which he had assumed power only as a "credibility problem."

A key aspect of the Reagan administration's willingness to work with Manigat was its stated belief that he would be able to move against repressive forces within the military. Deputy Secretary of State for Inter-American Affairs Richard Holwill articulated this view on March 23, 1988 in testimony before the House Subcommittee on Western Hemisphere Affairs when he spoke of the need to support Manigat if he took "strong action against certain members of the military." In reference to the November 29 killings, Secretary Holwill stated that "we would expect to see investigations and punishments." However, since Manigat lacked a base of support apart from the army, there was little likelihood that such a move would succeed. Indeed, Manigat proved unable to carry out even steps required by the Constitution -- separating the police from the army and holding local elections -- and when ultimately he attempted to assert authority over the army in June 1988, he was promptly ousted.

As noted, the Reagan administration's support for the Manigat government included an economic dimension which, while not technically prohibited by the legislated aid suspension, undercut the potential of that suspension to encourage reform. Needing approximately $7 million a month for imports of basic necessities, and with foreign reserves dwindling to approximately $10 million, the Manigat regime in the spring of 1988 faced the immediate prospect of being unable to import needed commodities. Rather than affirming its commitment to see new elections held in conformity with the Haitian Constitution, the administration stepped in and provided a $9 million loan guarantee to US exporters which permitted the Haitian government to purchase commodities and resell them at a profit, thus replenishing its treasury. The move was particularly inappropriate because death squads -- at least some of which, according to reliable reports, were composed of nonuniformed soldiers loyal to then Armed

Forces Commander-in-Chief Gen. Namphy -- had resumed regular murders of seemingly random targets in Port-au-Prince.

On June 19-20 1988, in response to efforts by Manigat to reshuffle the army's senior command, soldiers supporting Gen. Namphy overthrew Manigat. Namphy named himself president, rescinded the Constitution, and proclaimed the army the sole guarantor of democracy and human rights.

These blatant affronts to any pretense of democracy led the State Department to adopt a more disapproving tone. The State Department condemned the coup as a "serious blow to hopes for democracy" in Haiti, and noted that the conditions for the renewal of aid to Haiti were, among others, "strict observation of human and civil rights" and the establishment of a "credible transition toward a democratic and civilian government in Haiti."*

Despite this professed commitment to human rights, the Reagan administration remained mostly silent as violent abuses mounted, directed principally against opposition efforts to organize peasants in the countryside. For example, the administration said nothing in June and July 1988 when military and paramilitary forces machine-gunned and firebombed union offices in Gros Morne and St. Michel de l'Attalaye. Nor did it comment in August 1988 when a local section chief and others murdered four young members of a peasant youth organization in Labadie.

During an interview with our delegation in August 1988, US Ambassador to Haiti Brunson McKinley championed this policy of silence. When questioned about violent attacks on the right of assembly, Ambassador McKinley opined: "Human rights violations are endemic to the Haitian tradition. It's part of the culture. The way Haitians deal with robbers is stoning them to death. We

---

*   The United States Trade Representative (USTR) also agreed in July 1988 to review two petitions, filed by the AFL-CIO and the United Electrical Workers, challenging Haiti's eligibility for trade benefits under the Generalized System of Preferences (GSP) because of labor rights violations. The petitions were filed pursuant to the US Trade Act, which provides that country recipients of duty-free treatment for certain exports under GSP must demonstrate that they are taking steps to afford workers internationally recognized labor rights, including freedom of association and the right to organize and bargain collectively. The USTR heard testimony on the petitions in November 1988, and is expected to decide whether to suspend Haiti's GSP benefits in April 1989.

may not like it but its their tradition." When asked about a pattern suggesting a policy of official tolerance or complicity in violent abuses, particularly in the countryside, Ambassador McKinley responded: "Most things that are done by the Haitian government are done by gosh and by golly, and often by hazard. I don't see any evidence of a policy against human rights, any more than they have a policy about anything else." He added: "The countryside is out of control of the Haitian government. It's pretty primitive out there."

When asked what influence the US embassy might be able to exert to press for an improvement in the perilous human rights situation, particularly in the countryside, Ambassador McKinley observed: "Our ability to affect events in the countryside ended in 1934 [the year that US Marines left Haiti]. Since then, it's been the law of the jungle out there. There's no system of justice, no recourse, no education, no anything." When asked why he rarely protested human rights abuses, Ambassador McKinley commented that "anyone can make a statement about human rights. You can't accomplish anything sitting around the Foreign Minister's office.... Repetition becomes boring."

Despite this contemptuous attitude toward human rights issues in Haiti, Ambassador McKinley trumpeted the US embassy as "the biggest human rights organization in Haiti." And while conceding that he had made no effort to contact Haitian human rights groups, he complained that these groups had not come to see him.

The Reagan administration's silence finally was broken in the aftermath of the September 11, 1988 attack on St. Jean Bosco church. The State Department "condemn[ed]" the violent attack; called on the military government to "investigate, apprehend and punish" the attackers; and noted the government's responsibility for ensuring the security of its citizens.

Following the September 17, 1988 coup which ousted Gen. Namphy and brought Gen. Avril to power, the administration struck an initially cautious tone. It was careful not to read too much into certain promising statements and symbolic steps of the Avril government, but insisted that these gestures be followed by concrete actions. Responding to vows by Gen. Avril to respect human rights and to begin a dialogue with the democratic opposition on holding new elections, a US embassy spokeswoman opined: "We consider his themes to be very hopeful. But we are waiting to see what kind of actions this government takes to put them into effect."* State Department spokesman Charles Redman announced that the US was "encouraged" by such developments as the formation of a largely civilian cabinet, but he stressed that aid would not be renewed until the new government had acted to fulfill the longstanding US conditions of strict respect for human rights and the establishment of a credible transition to civilian, democratic rule. These guarded statements provided the democratic opposition with crucial support in its effort to press the Avril government to undertake promised political reforms.**

Congress assisted the Reagan administration's steadfastness by enacting legislation which extended the aid suspension for another fiscal year. In a non-binding resolution, Congress also urged restoring the March 1987 Constitution, appointing a "genuinely independent electoral commission to oversee elections," announcing a date certain for elections, "strictly observ[ing]" human and civil rights, disarming and restraining the Tontons Macoutes, instituting a judicial process whereby "human rights violations will be vigorously investigated and violators will be brought to justice," and "demonstrat[ing] the willingness of the Haitian armed forces to submit to legally constituted civilian authority and to fully respect and abide by the Constitution."

Unfortunately, the Reagan administration soon began signaling that it would consider renewing aid before these steps had been taken, if only Congress would agree. As reported above, the administration obtained informal

---

*   Julia Preston, "New General Installed Following Haitian Coup," The Washington Post, September 19, 1988.

**   The Administration also played a constructive role in preventing Col. Jean-Claude Paul from securing the post of armed forces commander-in-chief -- a post which would have been particularly inappropriate given the long history of human rights abuses by troops under Paul's command. As noted, Paul later was removed as commander of the powerful Dessalines Battalion and soon died under circumstances suggestive of poisoning.

agreement from key members of Congress for another loan guarantee, this time permitting the sale of $10 million of basic commodities to the Haitian government. Again, by reselling the commodities, the government generated revenues which relieved the mounting financial pressure to establish democracy and respect human rights.* With the incentive to reform significantly reduced, the Avril government has proceeded on the increasingly troubling path outlined in this report.

In addition to this important financial support, the State Department became an apologist for the Avril government's human rights record with the issuance of its *Country Reports on Human Rights Practices in 1988*. Released to the public on February 8, 1989, the report was completed before the Reagan administration left office on January 20, 1989, with Ambassador McKinley and the US Embassy in Port-au-Prince principally responsible for the factual material contained in the report. Although the report described a range of abuses committed under the CNG and the Manigat and Namphy governments, it virtually whitewashed the human rights record of the Avril government. For example:

- It stated that "[t]he first three governments which held power in Haiti in 1988 (from January 1 to September 17) failed to defend effectively the human rights of the populace...," implying that the fourth government, the Avril government which took power on September 17, did defend human rights.

- Similarly, it asserted that "[p]olitically motivated killings, mistreatment of prisoners, and arbitrary arrests and detention took place in Haiti before the coup which unseated the Namphy Government," again implying that all this had changed following Gen. Avril's rise to power.

- And again, it reported that "before the September 17 coup, bands of thugs attacked people and institutions with the apparent purpose of

---

*   Also as discussed above, the Administration released approximately $15 million worth of gourdes, the Haitian currency, which were the proceeds of the CNG's earlier sales of food donated by the Administration under the PL 480 program. US law governing such proceeds gave the Administration little choice but to release the money to be spent on a series of development programs and other projects agreed to by the Haitian and US governments.

preventing the exercise of basic rights," as if this phenomenon were unknown under Gen. Avril.

- The report referred to the Haitian Constitution of 1987 as if it were still
  an active instrument, such as by stating that Gen. Namphy "ignored,"
  rather than rescinded, the Constitution, and by referring to various sections of the Constitution as if they were still in force. The result was to
  relieve Gen. Avril of the obligation to restore the Constitution, a step
  he so far has refused to take.

- And the report took the Avril government's word for things which are
  either demonstrably false or for which there was no independent
  evidence. Thus, the report asserted, contrary to fact, that "Recherches
  Criminelles ... was made into a purely investigative police facility," and
  it stated, despite a lack of corroborative evidence, that "the Avril
  Government announced that it had taken into custody four suspects
  accused of participation in the 1987 murder of presidential candidate
  Yves Volel." Similarly, the report observed that the Avril government
  "ordered the closing of Fort Dimanche," without noting that the closure
  has not yet occurred.*

Needless to say, the persistent and serious abuses detailed in the chap-
ters above belie the State Department's rosy picture of the Avril government's
human rights record. The State Department's eagerness to portray human rights
under Gen. Avril in this falsely positive light suggests a willingness to color the
facts in order to facilitate easing the restrictions on US aid to the Haitian government. Democracy and human rights in Haiti will be the victims if this policy of
deception prevails. The Bush administration has an opportunity to avoid a
repetition of the failed policy which led to the massacre and aborted elections
of November 29. It can do so only by stressing, as current legislation requires,
that high-sounding pronouncements and superficial reforms will not suffice to
renew aid. It must stress that aid in any form will not flow until human rights are
respected and free and fair elections -- not sham elections of the sort that
brought Manigat to the presidency -- are held in accordance with the proce-

---

* Along these same lines, State Department spokesman Charles Redman stated on November 7, 1988 that the Avril government had "arrested some Tontons Macoutes alleged to
  have been involved in the election massacre of November 1987." We are at a loss to know
  what he was talking about.

dures outlined in the Constitution. (The sole possible exception should be small amounts of aid used exclusively to fund the electoral process, such as aid to fund a genuinely independent electoral commission.) To make new elections safe and meaningful, the Bush administration should also press the Haitian military to disarm paramilitary forces; to defend and support the electoral process, including by apprehending and prosecuting those responsible for gross abuses of the past; and to respect election results regardless of outcome. Renewing aid before these conditions are met will undercut the main source of leverage that the democratic opposition has to force a break with Haiti's Duvalierist legacy.